To Kevin.

Best wishes

BOB LENARDUZZI

BOB LENARDUZZI

A Canadian Soccer Story

Bob Lenarduzzi

and

Jim Taylor

HARBOUR PUBLISHING

Harbour Publishing Co. Ltd.
P.O. Box 219, Madeira Park, BC, V0N 2H0
www.harbourpublishing.com

Cover photograph by Nick Didlick
Edited by Ian Whitelaw
Cover design by Anna Comfort
Text design by Mary White
Index by Ellen Hawman
Printed and bound in Canada

Harbour Publishing acknowledges financial support from the Government of Canada through the Canada Book Fund and the Canada Council for the Arts, and from the Province of British Columbia through the BC Arts Council and the Book Publishing Tax Credit.

Library and Archives Canada Cataloguing in Publication

Lenarduzzi, Bob, 1955–
    Bob Lenarduzzi : a Canadian soccer story / Bob Lenarduzzi and Jim Taylor.

Includes index.
ISBN 978-1-55017-546-2

    1. Lenarduzzi, Bob, 1955–. 2. Soccer players—Canada—Biography. 3. Soccer coaches—Canada—Biography. I. Taylor, Jim, 1937– II. Title.

GV942.7.L45A3 2011   796.334092   C2011-904627-X

*For Deanne, who's been there
through good times and bad,
and made soccer my second-greatest passion*

CONTENTS

PROLOGUE . . .

So why the book? Good question.

Maybe because I will talk soccer with anyone, anywhere. Always have, always will, partially to promote the sport, partially because when two soccer fans get together the topic kicks in almost instantly. In the process, old memories bob to the surface: the fun times, the sad times, the laughter, the madcap, unbelievable North American Soccer League (NASL) days when the original Vancouver Whitecaps took the city by storm and by the heart.

Maybe, too, because the Whitecaps have launched this incredible new adventure, this step up into Major League Soccer (MLS), and from first kickoff their fans—old-timers, first-timers and newcomers who've heard the buzz and decided that something big could be happening—have accepted and supported it so wholeheartedly that I can close my eyes and believe it's 1979 again and hear the cheering thousands singing as we ride open cars through the downtown streets, waving the Soccer Bowl . . .

> *"White is the colour, soccer is the game;*
> *we're all together, and winning is our aim . . ."*

Maybe because so many of the people now crowding into Empire Field in our first MLS season weren't around in those days, or are too young to have heard the stories of those often-magical times in the NASL when, for a couple of years at least, the Whitecaps were a force in the local market along with the hockey Canucks and football Lions—as I believe they will be again.

Yes, I'm biased. I've been part of this team in its various incarnations for the majority of my life as player, coach and executive, and now as president of the most ambitious project in BC soccer history, so how can I not be biased? But I believe those stories are too good, too heartwarming and funny to be locked away in memories or as headlines and clippings in fading and forgotten scrapbooks. Today's players, so much better off in every aspect of their sport, should know how it was back in the day. They should hear about the games and the talented, competitive, sometimes zany people who played them.

Jim Taylor was there for so much of it. He travelled with the national team to Newfoundland for the improbable quest for a World Cup berth, and through Central America when similar quests were doomed to failure. He has known me since I was nineteen. When we meet, we laugh a lot and the old tales and names click in like it was yesterday—Ginger Pickburn, "King" Kevin Hector, Alan Hinton, Willie Johnston, Alan Ball, John Best . . . so many more.

In a sense, this book might be an excuse to go back and relive those wonderful, improbable days as we look ahead to those to come. Taylor tells me that Thomas Wolfe wrote that "you can't go home again." Maybe not to stay, but there's nothing to say we can't drop back for a visit . . .

1

YOU'RE FIRED!
WELCOME BACK!

Whenever it is in any way possible, every boy should choose as his life's work some occupation that he should like to do anyhow, even if he did not need the money.
—Irish blessing

In a crazy way, I guess you could say that the Vancouver Whitecaps' move into Major League Soccer began the day team owner David Stadnyk fired my ass.

Step back a bit: The original Whitecaps had been gone for eleven seasons, along with the rest of the North American Soccer League. After two soccer-less summers a new franchise called the Vancouver '86ers emerged from the ashes in 1986 to compete in a new Canadian Soccer League. I'd coached them from '87 to '93, also coaching the men's national team for two years, left them to devote myself full-time to the nationals in 1994 and came back as general manager in '97.

On the field the '86ers were a big success—revenue-wise, not so much, which led to a string of owners, the latest being Stadnyk. He took over in 2000, made an agreement with the club's ex-director John Laxton to use the Whitecaps name, and then bailed on the club midway through the 2002 season. Not, however, before he'd fired me after an argument over how the club should be run.

Confused? Hang in there. It gets better.

The league, on the hook to pay the bills to complete the season, asked me to come back to run things and look for a new owner. It was not a fun job. Several people expressed interest, but they were a bunch of tire kickers, curious in the beginning but quick to shy away from the considerable financial commitment. I was working for nothing, just trying to keep things afloat, but we were nearing the end of the season and I was thinking, jeez, this thing could be *over*.

I got a call from a guy named Mark James, owner of a local clothing store and restaurant. Mark's wife, Ally, was an avid soccer player and a big supporter of the women's team. When she read of our problems, she convinced Mark to give me a call.

"I've got this guy," he said. "I think you should phone him. He could be interested."

Well, I'd about had it with all the Toms, Dicks and Harrys calling and thinking they had the answer. I was tired and I was jaded.

"I don't want to be calling people hat-in-hand to sell them on this," I told him. "They have to know they're not going to be making money and need to look at it as a long-term investment."

Mark could have said "Fine," hung up and forgotten about it. Heaven bless his patience.

"How about *I* call him?" he suggested. "I'll tell him that, give him your info and see if he's interested. It can't hurt."

He made the call, then called back to tell me that this Greg Kerfoot guy said that if it turned out he *was* interested, he'd call me by Friday.

Greg Kerfoot? Who in blazes was Greg Kerfoot?

The call came the next day. "Come over and see me on Monday," he said. "I'd like some more information."

Well, he was interested enough to make the call, which put him a step ahead of a lot of the looky-loos who'd preceded him. But who *was* he? I'd not heard his name anywhere in the soccer community or anywhere in the sporting world, period. And I'd already made it clear it was going to be a money-losing proposition for the foreseeable future.

As I came to learn, the answer was pretty basic, as was Kerfoot himself. He was a computer software developer who'd launched a company with two or three employees, built it into a major player in the industry and sold it for one of those figures that have so many zeros in front of the decimal point that you lose track. He'd made his money here. Now he wanted to give back to the province and to the city. The Whitecaps had been a major part of the BC sports scene. Now they were in danger of folding. Hence, the call.

Our meeting was at 9 a.m. I'm still there at 3 p.m. and we've gone for lunch in between.

I'm a real believer in first impressions, and this quiet guy seemed genuinely interested. He wasn't going to leap in. In the three weeks before the league meeting that would be our last if we couldn't find new ownership, we fed him info on budgets and all aspects of the club's operation. Meanwhile, he called people in the sport such as Milan Ilich, who'd financed the team in the early going, asking, among other things, about me.

I was at the Burnaby Lake soccer complex standing behind one of the goals when my cell phone rang. It was Kerfoot calling from Hawaii, where he was vacationing.

"You know what?" he said. "I think I'm going to do this."

It was so matter-of-fact that I wasn't entirely sure what he meant.

"You mean, you're going to get involved?"

"Yeah, I think I will."

It was strange at the time, but as I came to know him I realized it was typical of him. He'd done his due diligence and was ready to go, but he wasn't going to make a big deal of it. For me it was one of those where-were-you-when-JFK-was-shot moments, so vivid that I remember him saying "Yeah" and thinking "Wow!" But I had no idea how significant his decision would be, because he'd given no indication of what sort of investment he was going to make or how long he'd be in.

Nonetheless, we started up shortly thereafter and I ran headlong into another facet of this man who by now had agreed to take over the entire operation. His decision was big news and we needed the publicity, so I called a press conference to spread the word.

"I won't be coming," he said.

"But . . . but, it's about you taking over the team," I protested. "The media are going to want to *talk* to you!"

"I know," he said. "But you can tell them."

And that was that.

Nothing has changed. From that day to this, through the move to the United Professional Soccer League and now to the MLS, despite all he has done to promote soccer at every level—so many things that to list them would take an extra chapter—Greg Kerfoot has remained a background guy who treasures his privacy, refuses all requests for interviews, sits unnoticed in the stands with a baseball cap putting his features in shadow and politely declines newspaper and TV photographers' bids for even a mug shot.

I can bear witness to that. Early in our first season we would sit together in the stands watching the game, preferably away from the crowd. On one occasion we were so far back in the Swangard Stadium bleachers we were practically in the street, the only two people in the section. Suddenly Greg notices a guy using a zoom lens and pointing right at Greg.

I went over to check it out and told him we'd really prefer he didn't take the shot. "Just doing my job," he said pleasantly. "I'm with the *Sun* and they want a shot for a feature they're running on Mr. Kerfoot."

For me, that presented a huge problem. I knew Greg was serious about the privacy issue. What if he got ticked off at all the media interest and *pulled out of the soccer operation*?

There had to be a way out of this. Think, Bobby. *Think* . . .

They wouldn't have a personal interview with Greg, because he'd never allow it. That meant the feature would be put together by talking to other people. Maybe I could talk them out of using a photo. I called the *Sun* the next day and explained the situation. They didn't laugh, I'll give them that. But the picture ran, crystal clear and maybe half a page deep. And there was a consequence: Greg stopped sitting with me at games. "You're well known by the sports crowd," he explained. "If you're too close, if they see you with me, they'll figure it out."

It's been tough convincing the media that Greg is serious about his privacy. "He owns the *team*," they plead. "Surely to God you could set it up."

I try. I tell Greg that this reporter or that one is a great guy who'd do a fine job. His answer is "Okay, he's a great guy. But I'm still not doing the interview." Having taken a stand from the start, he clearly feels that if he does one interview, it will open the floodgates.

In the light of what the man has done for the team and the sport, we're hardly about to complain, because when he said he was in, he most definitely meant all the way.

He took over officially on November 13, 2002, a guy in his early forties clearly not into time wasting. Our first office was in a house next door to his home in West Vancouver. We started with three people and Greg began working his way through the learning process in the business of professional soccer. He added a marketing person, then a communications person. The operation got too big for the house so we moved into downtown offices. In a short time the staff rose to fifteen. As the MLS season opened, the number stood at sixty-plus, without an ounce of fat.

Sometimes, he caught me flat-footed.

One day a couple of months into the operation he asked me where the team trained.

"Clinton Park, where I played my minor soccer."

"Where's that?"

"East Vancouver."

"But that's a public park," he said.

Yes, I agreed, and actually we were at the bottom of the pecking order for field use as the community groups rightly got first crack at the good times and we had to take what was left because there weren't too many alternatives.

He thought about it for a few seconds. Then:

"We should look into building our own training centre."

For me, that came out of left field, but Greg sent out letters to the various municipalities asking who'd be interested in being part of constructing such a site. We're still looking. We have some government funding and Greg's commitment but we still don't have a municipality willing to jump in. Go figure.

At a time when we'd already proved how difficult it is to find serious investors with serious money to put into the game's development, here's a guy who built two on-campus soccer pitches—at a cost of roughly $5 million—at Simon Fraser University to provide us with a place to train, even though there wasn't enough land for a training centre. He also committed $1 million to the women's national team and brought them together in Vancouver in a residency program so they could train together and have a legitimate chance at the Olympics and the last World Cup, even though it meant our own women's team would lose some of our best players for that period, and he offered to build a 20,000-seat stadium on the waterfront. And no one with the clout to get it done is willing to step up?

Truth be known, I'm not sure Greg was all that interested in trying for an MLS franchise at first. Our objective from the beginning was to be a good team in the USL, and we accomplished that. In 2005 our men's and women's teams both won league titles, and to Greg one was just as satisfying as the other. From the beginning, two long-term philosophies were firmly in place: the women's team was not a token addendum to the organization, it was part of it; and we would have to partner with the BC minor soccer system, because the only way our local talent would evolve to a future place on our club was if we developed it.

When it came to looking ahead or putting new ideas into play, Greg had a three-pronged criteria process. Would it: (a) help us progress to our goal of becoming one of the best small-market franchises in the world; (b) be a significant community asset; and (c) help to grow the sport in BC and in Canada? If a plan or project hit two of them, fantastic, but it had to hit one or it was scrapped.

At the time the MLS rumblings surfaced, the aim for our men's team was to be successful at our own level, then upset Toronto to win the Nutrilite Cup and qualify for the Confederation of North, Central American and Caribbean Association Football (CONCACAF) playdowns. Then word came through the jungle drums that Francesco Aquilini, owner of the NHL Vancouver Canucks, wanted to bid for one of the two expansion franchises to which the MLS was committed. He'd been talking to his friends in Toronto, where the team was pulling in crowds of about 20,000, thought it could work here, and reportedly had launched a preliminary strike with secret talks with MLS commissioner Don Garber. Earlier, he'd contacted Greg to inquire about the possibility of a joint venture.

One thing was certain. There was no room in Vancouver for two soccer franchises, and that left Greg with a set of choices that he presented to me and to Rachel Lewis (who'd been brought in to handle the business end of our operation) to think about over the weekend: join the Aquilini bid; put in our own bid; or step aside, let him have it, and essentially fold our tent.

The decision was unanimous. I'm pretty sure that even if it hadn't been, Greg would have gone for it anyway. He's a scrapper, we'd put a lot into the game, and the idea of bowing out and letting Aquilini have it didn't sit well. We would launch a bid of our own.

Say it quickly enough and it doesn't sound like that big a deal, but the North American pro soccer scene had changed dramatically since that day in the early '70s when Herb Capozzi bought Vancouver an NASL franchise for $25,000. Toronto FC's executives had to cough up a *$10-million* franchise fee to join the MLS in 2007. With the success of that franchise and of the league itself, we knew our franchise might cost double or even triple that. Stepping up in class would require a higher calibre of on-field talent, which would not come cheaply and could add at least a couple of million to the investment—a lot of money, particularly when Greg and his partners wouldn't have total control of it.

I have to admit, my own reaction to the formation of the MLS was initially one of skepticism—NASL memories perhaps, or a recurring itch from old battle scars. When the MLS launch, scheduled for 1995 with twelve teams, was put on hold for a year with the announcement that there were issues still to be decided and things still to be put in place, I was all here-we-go-again, more promise without delivery, and now they've lost the momentum generated by the '94 World Cup.

As it turned out, they'd done exactly the right thing, and the way they did it was an indicator of the way things were going to be: commitment, long-term planning and the guts to correct mistakes quickly rather than letting them fester. At the end of the 2001 season, for example, when it became apparent that the two Florida franchises were drawing neither customers nor interest, they were terminated. Poof, gone. Lose two limbs, but save the patient.

The decision was consistent with the league's structure and philosophy: the MLS operates as a single entity. It owns the player contracts, takes a cut out of gate receipts and sets a team salary cap ($2.85 million this year) to avoid the bear trap of some team owner getting stars in his eyes and going out to buy success no matter what the cost. That strategy never works, but teams and leagues have folded because one or two tried it. There is no doubt about who has control of the MLS.

I wasn't the only skeptic—they were everywhere. Single entity hadn't worked in the United States Football League. MSL players had given in to the concept only after a bitter court fight, so why would this be any different? The answer was financial support—really *big* financial support—from the Hunt Sports Group (think Lamar Hunt, the American Football League, World Championship Tennis, the NBA's Chicago Bulls and too many other sports ventures to mention), from the Kraft Sports Group and from the Aschutz Entertainment Group (AEG), all of whom had faith in the game and its North American future and had decided to bankroll it until it took root.

At one time AEG owned six MLS franchises—Colorado Rapids, the MetroStars of New Jersey, DC United, the Chicago Fire, Los Angeles Galaxy and the Houston Dynamos. The Hunt group owned the Columbus Crew, the Kansas City Wizards and the Dallas Burn. Kraft (think the NFL's New England Patriots) owns the New England Revolution, which now plays, as do the Patriots, in the 68,756-seat Gillette Stadium. Franchise shifts and sales have altered the ownership map, but the backing is still rock solid. When AEG sold the MetroStars to Red Bull, the energy drink people, the *New York Times* reported the price "in excess of $300 million."

As for the Hunt Group, which now owns the LA Galaxy and part of the Houston franchise, there is no indication of any waning of the enthusiasm and commitment for the game that Lamar Hunt, who passed in 2006, had shown since that day in 1962 when he and his future wife, Norma, attended a Shamrock Rovers' game in Dublin. Talk about instant love. He attended the World Cup in England in 1966—and nine of the next eleven. For three of them (1994 in the US, 1998 in France and 2002 in Korea and Japan) he attended at least one game in every World Cup stadium. Without men like him, the MLS might never have survived its initial growing pains. But look at it now.

One thing had changed in our own operation. Greg now had some heavies with him. NBA star Steve Nash, whose brother Marty played for us and for the national team, and Steve's Victoria high-school buddy Jeff Mallett, former president and chief operating officer of Yahoo, were both soccer nuts and had phoned Greg asking about a possible partnership.

It was a great fit. The entire Nash family was into the sport. Basketball was naturally No. 1 with Steve, but he'd been a fine soccer player and still loved to get into pick-up games. Jeff was a 5'4" striker who spent two years in Canada's national program as a teen-ager—"I was the sneaky little guy up front." They were welcomed, as was American Steve Luczo, part owner of the NBA's Boston Celtics. It wasn't just money they brought to the table—it was a commitment by like-minded people with a common goal.

We threw a press conference and announced that we were putting in a franchise bid, but it wasn't just a press conference. It was also a pre-emptive strike to get our bid established in the public mind while simultaneously blowing any potential Aquilini bid out of the water. We had civic and provincial politicians in attendance, including premier Gordon Campbell. We had radio, television and newspaper reporters and columnists there by the dozen. There was no animosity. The Aquilini group had every right to launch its own bid, but with the big local names already seen to be lining up with us, it wouldn't be easy.

They must have thought so, too. In the end ours was the only Vancouver bid, and in March 2009 the MLS selected the Whitecaps and Portland to open in 2011.

Now, this ain't my first rodeo. I have seen soccer dreams, teams and leagues collapse before, but there's no worry niggling at the back of my mind this time. Ask Greg how long he'll be involved and he says, "Forever." He is not being flippant. The new Whitecaps are here to stay.

Once in a while, thinking back on how it's evolved, I want to pinch myself, remembering the twelve-year-old chasing balls at Callister Park or bouncing them off walls or garage doors when the summers went on forever and the dreams were limitless.

And I ask myself how anyone could be this lucky . . .

2

YOU WANT TO GO WHERE???

"When he says he wants to go, just thinking about it I cry so much my eyes get sore."

—Clelia Lenarduzzi

So there I was, fresh from my first ever plane flight, standing at the entrance to Elm Park—home of Reading FC for the past *73 years*, for Pete's sake—in no way ready to launch my professional soccer career but determined to do it anyway. I was fourteen years old, and my life was about to change forever.

But what was I *doing* there, a kid from East Vancouver who'd never been farther from home than Powell River, BC, with some crazy idea that I could survive in England, the very home of the game I loved, a country loaded with kids my age who had the same dream and a hell of a lot more experience? Sure, it had seemed like a great idea, sitting at home in my living room browbeating my parents into letting me go. But now I was *there*. Now I'd have to *do* it: show enough to stick as an apprentice to begin with, and then do well enough in training to earn a shot at actually playing in the Reading youth and reserve teams. Suddenly, East Vancouver was a million miles away . . .

There still are people who write off East Vancouver as a rough neighbourhood, which I'll never understand. To me, it was heaven. Our house was half a block from the Pacific National Exhibition grounds, where the seventeen-day carnival was held every year with all its rides, games and shows, and the same distance from Callister Park, the Mecca of soccer in Greater Vancouver and my second home in the playing months between too wet and too cold. For a bruised-shins kid with soccer dreams dancing through his head, what could be better than that?

In these days of artificial turf, ultra-organized leagues and kids who don't understand the term "pick-up game," Callister Park would be a bit of a joke. Not a blade of grass to be seen. Games on a dirt surface that the rain turned to mud in nothing flat, often played the day after a night demolition derby or truck rally. Then you played through the ruts missed by Eddie Lay, the groundskeeper who lived in a room under the stands (fans grew used to seeing his laundry hanging from the underside bleacher supports) and tried his best to smooth the playing surface with a broom pulled behind a tractor.

The games were not what you'd call all that sporting. Put Columbus against Firefighters and you could almost guarantee at least one fist fight and the occasional police presence to cool tempers or save the referee. There was a grass field, but it was outside the building and slanted to such a degree that you played like those mythical cows that grazed on hillsides—the "sidehill gougers"—and, legend insists, had to be milked at a 45-degree angle.

I was a ballboy at Callister from as far back as I can remember. It got me close to the game and to the big guys who were playing. But that wasn't my only edge. The others were my two older brothers, Vanni and Sam, and later my younger brother, Danny. Vanni and Sam gave me a gift beyond price: they let me hang out with them and play in the pickup games. I wasn't treated like "Okay, he's our brother. Pick him last and we'll stick him in goal," although for a while I wanted to be a goalie because I liked diving around in the dirt. I had some skill for my age, and they let me play as an equal. I was always with them, and there was always a ball. If I came

From the time I could walk there was always a soccer ball to boot or keep someone else from booting, as here for Grandview Legion in a Provincial Cup final. *VANCOUVER SUN*

home from school and no one was around, I'd spend hours kicking it against our neighbour's garage door.

It was like I was born to play and always knew it. When people asked what I wanted to be when I grew up, I didn't say "Gordie Howe." I said "a professional soccer player," which was kind of weird since Canada didn't have a pro soccer league or even a team. I just knew. If there was ever a doubt, it was erased one early morning when my dad, my brothers and I sat in our living room to watch the grainy black and white live telecast of the 1966 World Cup Final, England vs. Germany, before 98,000 fans in London's Wembley Stadium.

I didn't realize it was a game of historic importance, that books would be written about it as German and English fans—and their children and children's children—argued over what the camera did or didn't prove. I just sat there, entranced, as England's Geoff Hurst scored three goals in a much-disputed 4–2 victory.

I'd learn the rest later: how Hurst's second goal came when his shot ricocheted off the crossbar and landed either onto or just beyond the goal line; how the Germans claimed his third should not have counted because elated English fans had swarmed onto the field before the shot was taken and how, years later, the Russian linesman who made the call on the goal line is said to have muttered on his deathbed, "Tell the Germans the ball was out, but I called it in anyway." (That last one is probably an urban myth, but I kind of like it.) All that mattered that morning was that I now knew beyond a doubt how I was determined to spend my life.

Flash forward to 1969. I'd come up though the minor soccer ranks with Grandview Legion, been selected runner-up to the Soccer Boy award at the annual *Vancouver Sun* provincial minor soccer tournament (Danny was named runner-up a few years later) and shown enough to get a call-up from a new men's team called the Vancouver Spartans. Adult soccer, and I had the ball. I'd just give this guy my best Grandview move and . . .

There probably was a thud, but I didn't hear it. One minute I

Reg Newmark and I still kid about it when we meet: sure, I'm with the Whitecaps—but who beat me out for the Soccer Boy award at the 1969 Sun Tournament of Champions? He did. Brother Danny was runner-up years later. *VANCOUVER SUN*

was starting my move and the next I was staring up at the heavens. The guy had put a shoulder into me and my fourteen-year-old body went airborne and landed with a thud that might have registered on the Richter scale. Welcome to the real world, kid. Any last requests?

It was a rude awakening. I was tall for my age, maybe 5'10", with a pretty good skill set, but I'd never been exposed to the game's physical side. Still, I must have shown something, because I was a regular at practice, and one fateful day my perseverance paid off.

Two kind and generous men with the Spartans at the executive level, John "Ginger" Pickburn and Bob Christopher, were always doing things to promote the game they loved. One night Ginger brought a guest to practice: Jack Mansel, coach of the Reading team in the English third division, who was vacationing in Vancouver. The next thing I knew, probably after a practice or two, Pickburn took me aside with a bombshell: Mansel had noticed me, he said, and wondered if I'd like to come to Reading and join the team as an apprentice professional!

My eyes widened. I could barely breathe. A chance to join an English FA club? Where did I sign? Okay, too young to sign. Parental permission? Fine! I'd go home and tell my parents I was going to England . . .

Oops.

You may think you understand the enormity of what I was about to ask of my parents. Unless you're Italian and grew up in the '60s, you don't.

Family was everything. Home wasn't a place where you slept when you weren't dashing off to hang out with your friends in a mall. Home was where you lived, the haven where your mom stayed home and ran the house while Dad was off to work, a sanctuary where the dinner table was not just a place to eat the marvellous meals she'd prepared, but the social hub where everyone discussed what had gone on during the day, how things were doing in the neighbourhood and what the plans were for tomorrow. There was talk and laughter, all part of a family fabric that was warm and loving and constant.

In Italy, my father, Giovanni, had been a cheese-maker. When he brought my mother, Clelia, and Vanni and Sam to the New World and settled in the house in East Vancouver, it was with two objectives: to give his boys an opportunity for a better education; and to find a job making cheese in his adopted country. When the second part didn't materialize, he found work at Palm Dairies. "Still making cheese," he'd joke. "Only, cottage."

He'd work from 6 a.m. to 4 p.m. and come home to that sit-down dinner. There was a continuity to it, something my wife, Deanne, and I have tried to emulate as we've raised our own kids. But in a world of mass and instant communication, a million things to do and television bringing in the world, it's not as easy as it was in that slower, calmer, more structured time.

It wasn't something I thought about. It just *was*. It wasn't until years later, in Italy with Team Canada, prepping for the '96 Olympics, that I truly learned the meaning of family roots. It started with what I can only call a duty trip. My dad had always been quietly disappointed that we'd never seen the place where he and my mom grew up. Now I was actually in the country and felt the obligation. I could see it: four days of staring at people I didn't know, trying to converse in a language I barely recalled . . . wonderful.

But a marvellous thing happened. I arrive at Codroipo, one of more than a hundred communes in the Friuli-Venezia Giulia region of Italy, bordering Austria and Slovenia, where I meet my aunt Delfina, my dad's only living sibling of eleven brothers and sisters. She's in her eighties, she's riding her bike, and when I see her I start to cry because she is my dad with hair.

It was almost spiritual. The more we chat over the next four days, the more the old language and dialect I'd heard from Mom and Dad as a child comes back. I'm hearing tales of my dad, I see the houses where he and Mom grew up and the cheese factory where he worked. Relatives gather, about forty of them, no doubt as curious

Our first home team: Mom and Dad, Clelia and Giovanni, were always there with love and support as Danny (R), Sam and I and our late brother, Vanni, pursued our soccer passion. LENARDUZZI COLLECTION

27

to see and hear "the American" as I was to listen to them. There's an accordion and wine and laughter. I can't remember having a better time.

And I hear a story that paints a picture and puts a lump in my throat. The tracks for the train carrying my dad off to war ran in front of my mom's house. As it chugged by, he waved and threw her a note. It said not to worry, that he'd be back to marry her.

My own kids have heard the stories now, and are interested in making the journey themselves. I like to think it's the call of the old blood, the call I'm forever grateful to have answered, and thankful that my dad lived to know that I did. The cancer was closing in on him. We had no idea how much time he had left, but I was able to retell the stories I'd heard, and even converse with him a bit in the old dialect, which I know was a proud moment for him.

Soccer was always a part of our lives, largely because of a happy accident. When my folks moved into the house in East Vancouver, they had no idea that Callister Park was practically next door. Dad went for a walk, heard the crowd noise and walked in to discover people playing the only game that mattered. Just like that, he was home.

On Sundays, the Italian community would gather for picnics in New Brighton Park. Once the food was eaten, washed down with homemade wine, the soccer balls would come out and within minutes there'd be a pick-up game. Skill was not a requirement. The ball came out, you played and laughed and shouted, nobody kept track of the score, and when it was over, both sides could claim victory. Good times.

My father was one of the wine-makers—and still a cheese-maker as well. He'd found a guy in Langley who had all the tools but none of the experience, so they made a deal: Dad would go to Langley to make the cheese, and his payment was in cheese rather than dollars. We ate a lot of cheese. Still do, still love it.

But, about the wine.

East Van was a solidly Italian community in those days and you could always tell when it was wine-making season because the local filling station would bring in a huge container of grapes that the locals would buy and convert into wine.

My father made wine for us and his buddies in the most archaic contraption imaginable. You put the grapes in the top, and they'd go down into the crusher, which must have been a hundred years old. It's still around somewhere. Maybe someday I'll dig it out. The crushed grapes would go down into the bottom part and sit there, and every day after work he'd squeeze them a little bit and the juice would flow through a little hole in the bottom into a container. It was an incredible process and one I looked forward to because you could eat the grapes as you threw them in, so we all got involved. Naturally, the kids at school all ribbed us about jumping into the vat barefoot to do the stomping, but what did we care? The grapes were great.

Then, one fateful year, there was the episode of the grappa.

You've never heard of grappa? Think "moonshine," a drink of lethal potency made from pomace, a term meaning the discarded grape seeds, stalks, stems and anything else left over from the regular wine-making process. It's been around since the Middle Ages, uniquely Italian and running 40–45 percent alcohol, a poor man's drink designed to get the farmers through the hard Italian winters. Generations of Italians have sipped it with meals or added it to their espresso to—and what a great Italian definition—"correct it."

Today, versions of grappa are produced by major distilleries all over the world for public sale, but when my father was making it, it was moonshine, concocted for home consumption by him and his buddies in the traditional manner of his upbringing. He wasn't selling it. My parents couldn't do anything deceitful—it just wasn't in them—but one of his "pals" must have ratted out him and his wine-making circle, because one afternoon there was a knock at the front door and there were the police.

They ransacked the house, even dug holes in the backyard, looking for the still that was making the grappa and, in particular, the grappa itself, which was pretty funny because it was sitting right there in the fridge while they searched.

Dad was charged and the case went to court. There was a picture in the *Vancouver Sun* of some of the equipment used, including a container Dad had brought home from work prominently displaying the Palm Dairies logo. You'd think it had been a major drug bust. I remember coming home and Mom was crying and asking, "How could this *be*?" It ended with Dad paying a fine—$100, as I recall, which doesn't sound like much now but in those days, for a working-class family, represented a pretty good smack on the wallet.

My mother never went to my minor soccer games, or my pro games, for that matter, although she'd listen to the Whitecap broadcasts. But she was into the process, all right. Dad would come home and tell her how we'd played, and he was pretty straight about it. He'd never get on me but if I hadn't played up to snuff he'd say something like "Not one of your best efforts." But if he came and told *Mom* we hadn't played well, she'd launch a tirade—not at us, but at him: "*You shouldn't say that! They're your sons!*" That never changed. In my first year with the Whitecaps I got red-carded and thrown out of a game, and all I could think of was "How am I going to explain this to Mom? She is gonna be *so* mad."

Life was simple and great. I had home, I had soccer, I had my brothers to play it with, and during the PNE I'd park cars on his front lawn for a guy down the street who charged a buck a park and gave me 25 cents per car as I jammed ten on the lawn and moved another in every time someone left. One year I made two hundred bucks.

Vanni, who passed away in 2000 at age sixty after a long bout with cancer, was the one who told me to use my left foot and showed me the mechanics of doing it. When people talk about the soccer Lenarduzzis, Vanni kind of gets overlooked because Sam, Danny and I all played in the NASL. The truth of it is, he may have been the best of us but the timing was wrong. When he was starring with Columbus in the Pacific Coast League there weren't all of today's opportunities. He could have played in the NASL in a heartbeat had it been operating. He must have been a good coach, too, because one of my best years with the Whitecaps was at left back and it was because I had a good left foot—thanks to my big brother.

Good things kept happening for me. One day at Callister I was ballboy and coach Joseph Csabai of the Eintracht club was short of players. He knew of me and knew I played, but I was thirteen years old. He handed me a jersey. "Go get changed," he said. He sat me on the bench and played me for the last ten minutes! For me, Callister was Wembley. I was put out wide at left wing and got a couple of touches. I was playing in the Pacific Coast League!

I rushed home to tell my father.

"You'll never believe it," I said. "I was *playing*!"

He started laughing and couldn't stop.

I had everything, and I was about to try to walk away.

I knew that getting the parental okay would require some heavy persuasion. So, naturally, I went at it in the silliest possible manner. "If you don't do this," I warned them, "I'm going to hold it against you for the rest of your lives!"

I was bluffing, of course. I was fourteen years old and living in an Italian culture in which a parent's word, particularly the mother's, was law. If they said no, what could I do? Get a paper route to save the air fare? Hope Mr. Mansel would wait until I turned eighteen? If my parents said no, it was no.

They went from no to maybe and finally to yes. In the end it was Sam who saved me. He was twenty and he had also caught Mr. Mansel's eye with the Spartans. My parents capitulated. If my older brother went with me, I could go.

They had just one other condition, a huge one for them: I would finish my high school education by correspondence. I agreed. I'd have agreed to anything. But I'm ashamed to say it didn't work out. I tried, but my life was being pulled in so many directions, all of them about soccer. There wasn't *time* for school work.

I could have made time. I should have. The fact that I didn't is my biggest regret. I did get some classes completed at Capilano College when I came home, but not enough. My parents had let me go to England at who knows what cost to them, and my thank you was to break my promise and set myself up as a shining example of what not to do. The fact that I made a good life can't bury that. I gave my word, and I broke it. There's never an excuse for that.

At fourteen, of course, that was the furthest thing from my mind. Just like that, we were on our way and ready to step over that Elm Park threshold into heaven knew what? But I didn't care. I was a professional soccer player! I'd be getting £10 pounds a week, which was (Ohmigosh!) $25! Plus room and board! Bring it on!

Elm Park was a ramshackle sort of place built in 1896, capacity 15,596 when I was there, and only 4,000 customers could sit down. The rest stood in terraces with a bar in front so they wouldn't fall into the row below. Such terraces are outlawed now and would never be considered in the soccer palaces erected over the last couple of decades, but in my time at Reading they were things to be loathed. After every match, the other two apprentices and I had to sweep them free of the garbage. Trust me, 12,000 customers could leave a lot of crap.

(The terraces were the birthplace of another of those soccer legends I love. It's said that once in your place it was impossible to squeeze down the line to get out to the loo or your place would be lost. So, it's said, you peed in the pocket of the man next to you. "Liverpool hot pocket," it came to be called, although Liverpudlians take no credit. Folklore, no doubt. One can only hope.)

Garbage clearance was just one of our jobs. We also had to clean and polish the players' boots and hang them on hooks every day, do the laundry, lay out the uniforms, sweep out the dressing room and generally be at the beck and call of anyone who wanted anything done. All this after morning training sessions and extra afternoon workouts at the whim of the coaching staff. In any other regimen the apprentice system would be called hard labour. In English football it was called "character building" and "testing a player's commitment."

Personal cleanliness apparently wasn't a priority. There was one shower and a huge bathtub into which all the players would plunge after game or workout. It was disgusting. I stuck to the shower until peer pressure ("Lookit the Canadian! Too proud to climb in here with the rest of us!") forced me into it. I got to know that tub very well, because it was our job to clean it every day. But at every opportunity I was back under the drippy shower.

Reading took some getting used to. It was a town of row housing, each unit so small you spent all your time in either the living room or your bedroom, which was really tough to get used to. TV soccer was on a delayed basis, matches cut to fit a one-hour time slot. The loneliness would get to me. In today's world, no problem: no matter where you are, there's the internet, Twitter, Facebook and all the other electronic gizmos. Communication is a finger-poke away. You know how many calls home I made from Reading? One a year, at Christmas. Too expensive.

The saving grace for me was the two women with whom I was billeted, Mrs. Bull and her adult daughter, Dorothy Waller, but adjustments were required on both sides. Take, for instance, the matter of the Brussels sprouts.

I had a healthy appetite and, let's face it, English cooking isn't the greatest. In that residence Brussels sprouts were a nightly dinner mainstay and I hated them, but was too polite to mention it in this new environment so I gulped and ate until, finally, I could stand it no more and had to admit my distaste for them. "Why didn't you *say so?*" Mrs. Bull asked, and from then on I was sprout free.

Sadly, there was only one Italian restaurant in town, and it wouldn't have lasted a day on Vancouver's Commercial Drive. I'd been raised in a home where my mom's life was cooking, and before I knew it that's where I was eating—at home. I broke my ankle in a kick-around at a local park in Reading and, just like that, Sam and I were back on the plane—me to heal, Sam because personal commitments were taking him back to Vancouver. His English soccer sojourn was over for good but apparently I'd showed something at Reading, because I was invited to come back when I got healthy—and once again Pickburn and Christopher were there for me.

When the ankle was mended they took me to the airport, my transportation paid. Before I boarded, Pickburn handed me an envelope. "You'll need this," he said. Inside was a handful of bills. I'd given no thought to money, or to anything else for that matter. All I knew was that I was going back to Reading to resume my soccer career. Even with all that help, I almost didn't make it.

At Heathrow airport, the Customs agent asked me why I was entering the country. "I'm going to play professional football," I said loftily.

"Work permit, please."

I had no paperwork. Nothing.

"I don't have one," I said.

Things got a bit iffy. I'm still not sure why they let me through. Certainly it wouldn't happen today. In the end maybe they figured a kid making up a story would come up with a better one than that. At any rate, I was soon heading for Reading in a car driven by Dennis Allen, whose career was just winding down. Maybe he was depressed about that or maybe he was just an average driver, because everyone over there drives like life isn't worth living. I'm sitting in what is, for me, the wrong side of a car racing down the wrong side of the road. There are no stop signs, because they're all roundabouts, and posted speed limits are viewed as minimums. It was the scariest 30 miles I've ever driven. When we pulled up in front of Elm Park it looked like heaven. I couldn't wait to get inside again, even if I'd soon be scrubbing out the bathtub.

Elm Park was both home and school for the next five years. I started off playing on the youth and reserve teams in regional competition, which was a big advantage because, geographically speaking, we were in an area that included first division clubs such as Chelsea, Arsenal and Tottenham and therefore we got to play against the youth and reserve clubs of first division powerhouses. I'd also get the odd game with the first team in the fourth division—more as my career progressed—but getting into those youth and reserve matches against the big first division sides was a huge advantage. No one watched us, but man, was it exciting.

When I think about it, the threads that tied my playing career together are amazing, as were the contrasts. In the Watney Cup pre-season tournament, open to the two top goal-scoring teams in each division in the previous season, Reading was drawn against Manchester United in their first game—and I'm sitting there in the stands looking out at legends: George Best, with his incredible ball skills and Broadway Joe Namath pizzazz; Dennis Law; Bobby Charlton . . . Two years earlier they'd won the European Cup against Benfica, and I'm there within touching distance. If anyone had suggested then that in a few years I'd be playing against Best in a professional league in North America, I'd have told him he was dreaming. In a League Cup early-round match against Burnley I was marking a young guy named Ray Hankin, who at that time was considered a real comer. Not many seasons later, he was my teammate in Vancouver.

I dressed for some memorable matches. I got in for the last twenty minutes of an FA Cup match against Everton at Goodison Park and had an unbelievable time—play-making, slide-tackling, the whole package. The next day a newspaper report praised my showing and said I should soon be challenging for a first-team spot.

But if cup competition matches had the danger of swelling a player's ego, the reality of league competition soon set that straight. We played in places such as Workington, Hartlepool, Crew and Chester, where visiting team accommodations were not what you'd call posh. To get into the bath in Chester you had to climb through a hole that had been smashed in the wall to avoid the expense of installing an actual door. It was like someone had taken a pick to it, and you could gash your bare hide on the jagged edges. When I came home between seasons, people would say "Wow, you're playing in England. What that must be like!" I never told them, because I wanted them to think it was better, but sometimes, oh my.

The dream, of course, was to get promoted to the first team, but in some ways there were times when playing on the youth or reserve teams was better. For one thing, you'd get more playing time. For another, being 30 miles from London, we played the reserves of the really big clubs like Arsenal, Chelsea, Tottenham and West Ham. And back then, egos weren't allowed. If you weren't on the big team you *did* play on the reserves, like it or not. Today guys have it in their deals that they don't have to.

Different days, those. On game day you could dress only twelve players, so teams didn't dress a backup goalie. If the keeper went down, they either handed the one sub the jersey and wished him luck, or moved one of the starters into the net and replaced *him* with the sub.

It's never easy for young players to crack the lineup. I knew that going in. What I didn't figure on was a nationality problem. I was a Canadian, and to English fans that was unfathomable. I think there'd been only two before me—Les Wilson with Wolves and Bruce Twamley with Ipswich—so they cut me no slack. Once, when I was struggling, a fan let me have it.

"Go back to Canada and play ice hockey, the way you're supposed to."

I made a big mistake. I acknowledged him by giving him the two-finger salute known over there as "the forks," but he topped me.

"Yeah," he yelled. "That's all you're worth: Two pounds!"

I put my hands over my head in surrender and yelled, "You win." Only an idiot does something to draw the British fans' attention. They're quick-witted, and once they get on you they're merciless. Lesson learned.

Back home, however, having a local boy in the English pro leagues was a big deal. When word got out that I might dress for an FA Cup match against Arsenal—featuring a future teammate named Alan Ball—it was a big story in the Vancouver press. In Reading they jammed 27,000 into Elm Park—how, I'll never know. I dressed, sat on the bench, and never got on the pitch. Next day, I was back sweeping the terraces.

The team with which you start your career always holds a special place in your heart, and I was particularly fortunate that mine was Reading. I can't speak for other English clubs, although I suspect it's probably true for them too, but at Reading there was a sense of community, the knowledge that no matter where you went you'd always be a part of the family. Years later I found this out first-hand, not once, but twice.

The man who assigned us the scut jobs—sweeping the terraces, scrubbing the tub, cleaning the equipment and anything else that might occur to him, was the groundskeeper, a man named Gordon Neate, who had been there forever.

In 1990 I took Deanne to Reading to see where it had all started and asked if Gordon was still around. He was cutting the grass. He saw me, shook his head, and continued mowing. When he got to us, he started telling Deanne stories about—with finger pointed— "this guy."

Shortly after Kerfoot took over the 'Caps, he and I went to Reading's brand new stadium—posh, as befitted a team now in the first division. But there was one constant: Gordon Neate was still there—last man on the groundskeeping staff now, but still a treasured and venerated employee and still so full of old Lenarduzzi stories that Greg's eyes started to glaze over. Family.

Reading thought I had potential. I knew that. I'd read the tabloid sports pages with the gossip about which clubs were eying which players, because I still dreamed of making one of the big clubs. As it turned out, the Reading brass had other ideas.

One day a man named Denny Veitch turned up representing a new Vancouver team called the Whitecaps, which would be launching a franchise in the North American Soccer League. I liked Veitch (which was fortunate, because in a few years he'd be my father-in-law), but how could anyone think seriously about a league whose initials made it sound like something coming out of a stuffy nose? If a guy was cut, was he post-NASL?

As it turned out, I'd get a chance to find out. In 1974, Reading sent me on loan to the Whitecaps. I was still going to play pro soccer, just as I'd always dreamed, but I'd be playing it at home.

3

MISSION IMPROBABLE

*"There are two blue lines, both of which are red.
Teams get points for losing unless they don't score any
goals in regulation time. But if the other team doesn't
score any either, then both sides get a chance for six
points . . . Welcome, then, to soccer's Brave New
World."*

— *Vancouver Sun*, May 27, 1974

The North American Soccer League was lightning in a bottle—early thunderous rumblings followed by a brief, dazzling flash of light so bright you'd swear it would last forever. The thing about lightning is it can hurt you, as it no doubt hurt a lot of NASL investors back when Commissioner Phil Woosnam trumpeted that *his* young and struggling league, not the National Football League, was going to be "the game of the '80s." But there's no substance—it's *all* flash, which would have been the perfect NASL obituary.

To be truthful about it, when Reading sent me to the Whitecaps on loan I viewed it almost like a holiday with the great fringe benefit that I'd be in my hometown. I'd play a couple of seasons, then go back to Reading and get on with my career, because just looking at the way the NASL was structured and the rules it had in place, you had to wonder.

They'd launched a new league for the most popular sport on the planet, a sport that over the centuries had survived rulings by assorted kings forbidding their subjects from playing it (Edward II and III, Richard II, Henrys IV, V and VIII, and James I, who ruled in Scottish parliament in 1424 "That nae man play at the Fute-ball." Even Elizabeth I got in on the act, ruling that men found playing soccer be jailed for a week. You can look it up.) So what did they do? They changed some of the rules.

"Americans want to see more scoring," they reasoned. "So let's give additional points for goals scored. And if the game ends tied, let's have a shootout, only none of that business of a guy standing at the penalty spot. Let's make them run at the ball from 35 yards out with five seconds to shoot and the goalie can't move until the kicker makes first contact with the ball. Won't that be *fun*!"

The determination to change the rules to accommodate goal-hungry Americans didn't end with the NASL. After the US was awarded the 1994 World Cup tournament (on the condition that it form a Division 1 national league, which led to the birth of the MLS), the US Soccer Federation sent Henry Kissinger to the 1990 tournament in Italy in an attempt to get the International Federation of Association Football (FIFA) to amend the rules for their event so American fans could relate. Among the suggestions: make the nets bigger, play four thirty-minute quarters, and eliminate the offside rule.

Mr. Kissinger must have known he was in tough. Before a press conference, with the world soccer media raging to get at him, he requested that they precede their questions by stating their country of origin "so that I may know from which direction the spears are being hurled."

FIFA ignored the requests, of course. The US staged its World Cup and made a tremendous success of it, and the MLS is now a vibrant and growing force. With the benefit of hindsight it's easy to laugh at the attempts to change the game, but as I joined the

Whitecaps, change was a reality that players, particularly those from soccer nations, found mind-boggling.

Six points for a win? Why? One point for each goal scored up to three, even if you lose? Why? After five games we had a 2–3 record and 18 points, which, a gleeful media pointed out, was more than the CFL's BC Lions had managed in any of their last eight seasons. How silly was it? On a night when we beat Boston 1-nil, we actually lost ground. We got 7 points, but Los Angeles got 9 for beating St. Louis 4–2 and Dallas got 8 for a 2–1 win over Philadelphia. We should have handed out calculators at the door.

As for the shootout, which is bad enough when done in the traditional manner from the penalty spot, it was too ludicrous to describe. Play through overtime to a draw, then lose on what amounted to a lottery that had nothing to do with reality or the game as it was intended to be played? Maybe in the US markets, where the game had yet to take hold, but in Canada, where touring teams had been playing international matches since 1885? In Vancouver, home of immigrants from soccer nations the world over who understood the game and liked it just fine as it had been for decades? Ridiculous.

But, okay, those were the rules. We'd live with them. We had a good bunch of lads, a likeable and knowledgeable Scottish coach named Jim Easton and a flamboyant, promotion-minded owner in Herb Capozzi. Now all we had to do was convince those soccer traditionalists that we were worthy of their support. Our problem was that too many of them clearly viewed this as a rerun of a movie they'd already seen and hadn't particularly liked.

Expansion in all sports had run rampant in the US, fuelled by the belief held by too many millionaires that a sports franchise could be run like a corner grocery and all they had to do was invest a million or so and sit back and watch the network television money pour in. Things got so ludicrous that not one, not two, but three different groups approached the US Soccer Football Association (USSFA) seeking permission to form a US professional league—permission that was needed because without the sanction of the Association and FIFA any player brought in would risk worldwide suspension.

One league was risky enough. Three competing leagues would be insane. When the three bidding groups couldn't get together the USSFA opted to choose one, and they picked the one fronted by Canadian Jack Kent Cooke. He had amassed his fortune in broadcasting and was now based in Los Angeles, where he owned the NBA Lakers and the NHL Kings and in 1967 had built the arena he dubbed The Fabulous Forum to house both teams. Cooke's all-time best quote was about Californians' refusal to support the Kings. He'd been told that there were more than 300,000 former Canadians living within a three-hour drive of Los Angeles. "Now I know why they left Canada," he said. "They hate hockey!"

He called his projected soccer empire the United Soccer Association, apparently feeling that USA would appeal to American patriotism. One of his twelve franchise sites was Vancouver, where local financing was available and fans had proved over the years that they'd come out to see touring clubs, a fact that convinced the league to trumpet that the franchise would average 20,000 fans in its first season. John Pickburn, who'd later make possible my move to Reading, would be general manager.

But there was a hitch: rather than scouting and signing individual players, the league decided to import entire teams for a twelve-game summer schedule. Vancouver got Sunderland, temporarily renamed the Vancouver Royal Canadians. And the party was on.

It wasn't that the club didn't play an exciting brand of soccer—there was talent there—but the Sunderland players saw the North American excursion primarily as an excuse to party. None did so with more enthusiasm than former Scottish international "Bacardi Jim" Baxter, who had a reputation for being able to drink himself senseless the night before a match, then play brilliantly in it. Of course, those stories tend to be exaggerated, but it is a fact that at age fifty-five, by then a non-drinking pub owner, Baxter required two liver transplants.

What happened, I suspect, was that the local fans were turned off by a sense of impermanence. The Sunderland club would go back to the English League at season's end, and then what? They stayed away in droves while the Royals won three, lost four and drew five. The projected 20,000 average ended at either 7,019 or more than 10,000, depending upon whether you believed the league stats or the newspapers.

At that the crowds looked tremendous compared to those of the ten-team outlaw National Professional Soccer League (NPSL) formed in a misguided burst of optimism that same year by the two groups who'd lost the USSFL bid to Cooke. The NPSL attendance was *topped* by Chicago at just over 6,000 per game. Undaunted, the league laid its survival in the hands of the courts, filing an $18-million anti-trust suit against the USSFL, FIFA and the rival USA.

Something had to be done. After much argument, threat and counter threat, the two leagues' twenty-two team owners decided to quit hating each other, in public at least, and amalgamate into the North American Soccer League. Media cynics in both leagues sneered and called it the Nasal. In one case, its press releases were dubbed "post-nasal drip." But in 1968, minus five teams from the disastrous previous season, the NASL launched to trumpets and the usual unbridled confidence.

In Vancouver the news was met with shrugs. Okay, the team name had been shortened to Royals, the rent-a-team concept was scrapped, and a big-name coach, Fulham's Bobby Robson, had signed a three-year contract and been given a $275,000 budget to bring in quality talent—laughable today, but impressive bucks in 1968. Among those the money bought were Huddersfield's Peter Dinsdale, Jon Green of Blackpool and Bobby Cram, coming off a great career with West Bromwich Albion. All told, an impressive start, but experience told would-be customers that something would go wrong, and something did.

The league decided to merge some of its teams rather than have two clubs in the same general area. Just like that, the San Francisco Gales, too close for comfort to Oakland, were merged with the Royals. However, the Gales already had a big-name head coach—Hungarian legend Ferenc Puskas, a.k.a. the Galloping Major, who spoke four languages, none of which was English. Naturally, he got the job and Robson went back to Fulham and on to English football fame and fortune.

Being twelve years old, I knew nothing about all the fuss and wouldn't have cared if I had. All I knew was that, whether they were Canadians or Royals, there was a team to watch. I went to all their games with my dad and would climb the fence at the old BC Lions practice field to kick the ball around and, when the Royals came out to train, to watch Puskas work out the goalies. The man was never fit and his playing days were long since over, but he could put the ball where he wanted—bend here, curve there, pick any corner he wanted. Unless he chose to give them some work, the only practice the poor goalies got was in waving as the ball went past.

The new Royals were hampered by owner George Flaherty, who had owned the Gales among many business interests, including the Ice Capades, but apparently saw no reason to provide the funds that Puskas loudly and publicly insisted he needed in order to bring in some scoring talent. The Royals finished dead last in the tough Pacific Division. Worse yet, they averaged only 5,900 fans in going 12–15–5 and scoring only 51 goals in thirty-two games. With the league reeling, what happened next was inevitable: the Royals folded, along with ten other teams, leaving the NASL on life support with a total of five franchises, the Park Avenue offices gone, the entire operation running out of two rooms in the basement of Atlanta's baseball stadium. "Put a tag on the big toe," the media said. "This baby is done."

In the next four years the NASL expanded, contracted and expanded again, spitting out failing franchises, taking on new ones and generally giving the impression that it had the life expectancy of milk in an open carton. Baltimore folded its tent, Rochester and Washington came in to make it a six-team league, Toronto and Montreal and New York Cosmos entered in 1971, but Kansas City was gone. A year later, the Washington franchise moved to Miami. Philadelphia Atoms arrived in '72 and promptly won the league championship, which so excited the NASL that it granted a whopping eight new franchises in 1974: Baltimore and Washington back for another crack at it, Denver, Boston, Los Angeles, San Jose, Seattle and—whadya know?—Vancouver.

All this, of course, I learned after the fact, checking out media histories and obituaries once I'd returned to Vancouver and was wondering just what the hell I'd gotten myself into. Given the city's professional soccer history with the Royals, there didn't seem to be a lot of reasons for optimism, but we had a weapon no other franchise possessed. We had Herb Capozzi, whose experience as former general manager of the BC Lions had taught him what little he didn't already know about how to play the media like a fiddle.

Yes, he enjoyed the limelight. Yes, he could dream up outrageous, attention-grabbing stunts. He once wrote an article for *Maclean's* magazine headlined "Canadians Play Lousy Football," an opinion the CFL found upsetting because (a) he *was* Canadian and (b) he'd played in the league for four years in Calgary and appeared in two Grey Cup finals with the Montreal Alouettes. In later years he turned up for a $10,000 challenge racquetball game against fellow sports entrepreneur Nelson Skalbania (the money to be used by the winner to build a racquetball court at the YMCA) accompanied by a Doberman on a chain and dressed as a Roman gladiator, except for the T-shirt bearing the message "Skalbania is just a poor country in the Balkans." Naturally, the media were out in full force.

Herb had been hired by Flaherty as "advisor" in the Royals' days, so he knew about the NASL's ongoing troubles. However, he'd been out of the sports spotlight since the Lions let him go in 1967, so when Dallas billionaire and NASL backer Lamar Hunt flew into town to talk to him about reviving the game in Vancouver he found a ready listener. Hunt's family, founders of the Okanagan's Calona Vineyards, had the money. Herb had the enthusiasm, the reputation and the know-how. The Whitecaps were born.

The name got unexpected attention, sparked by a media type studying Herb's gleaming smile and scoffing that we were the only team in history named after the owner's teeth. The truth of the matter was that Denny Veitch, Herb's pal and successor as GM of the Lions and now GM of the NASL franchise, was driving over the

Lions Gate Bridge one day when he noticed the white caps on the mountains and on the waves in the rough water, and came up with the ideal name for a BC franchise. Herb, though, took great delight in the media version, which he worked into his other hobby, as a brilliant, much-in-demand after-dinner speaker who used every opportunity to trumpet the Whitecaps' arrival and promise that we'd be great. Look out BC Lions. Look out Vancouver Canucks. Here come the 'Caps.

It was never going to be that easy—no one knew that better than Capozzi—but pro soccer was back in town. Now, the real work started.

4

GROWING PAINS

*"Soccer is the major sport in North America . . . We
have plans to expand to twenty franchises in 1975,
and to thirty-two teams in the next ten years!"*
—NASL Commissioner Phil Woosnam

The difference between Phil Woosnam and Herb Capozzi was
best illustrated by that old story about the woman who went to
charm school and learned to say "Fantastic!" instead of "Bullshit!"

No one believed in promotion more than Herb, but he knew
that there were limits to customer gullibility, and that to exceed
them was to invite ridicule. "Fantastic!" he could sell. Woosnam,
for all his hard work and good intentions . . . well, let's just say he
should have joined the woman in class.

It wasn't that he didn't know the game. A former Welsh schoolboy
international at striker, he left his job as a high-school physics teacher
at age twenty-six to turn pro with West Ham United, made 138 league
appearances and 106 more for Aston Villa, emigrated and became
player-coach for Atlanta Chiefs in the National Professional Soccer
League and head coach of the US national team in 1968. However, as
NASL commissioner, the man just wouldn't *shut up*.

When he flew into Vancouver before our second home game and made those ridiculous, pie-in-the-sky statements on the current and future status of the NASL, the ensuing media ridicule didn't merely mark him down as a carnival pitchman; it cut a chunk off what we'd already accomplished.

Yes, we'd lost our opener in the rain to San Jose, but we'd drawn 17,343 customers to Empire Stadium (thereby allowing Capozzi to win a bet he'd made with all the other Western Division leaders that we'd outdraw them on opening night). We'd ushered in the new team with bugles, bagpipes, cheerleaders and our foot-stomping, heart-pounding, adrenaline-pumping theme song, "The Sounds of Philadelphia," blaring through the warm-ups, and we'd played a crowd-pleasing, attack-minded style of soccer before unfortunately introducing our fans to the shootout tie-breaker and losing it 2–1.

We'd shown our fan base and 10,000 invited minor soccer players that we could and would entertain while offering them a

The side that started it all, the '74 Whitecaps. Back row (L to R): Rick Ragone (public relations), Bob Lenarduzzi, Doug Scorse, Gary Thomson, George "Dandy" McLean, Brian Budd, Neil Ellett, Brian Gant, Gerry Heaney, Billy Stevenson. Front: Harry Christie, Chris Bennett, Glen Johnson, Daryl Samson, Sam Nusum, Jim Easton (coach), Greg Weber, Bruce Wilson, Sam Lenarduzzi, Charlie Palmer, John Buchanan. BC SPORTS HALL OF FAME AND MUSEUM thoroughly professional product. The last thing we needed was the league commissioner making promises only an idiot would believe he could keep.

For the record, defender Neil Ellett scored our first ever goal, the ball somehow finding its way through a mass of players jammed in front of the net. (Where do the years go? Neil now sits close to me in the press box as referee assessor for our matches.) It was fitting that the historic goal should be scored by a Canadian, because Canadian talent, primarily products of the BC minor soccer program, made up much of our roster.

That was no accident. The way Capozzi saw it, fans who'd endured the Sunderland rent-a-team situation with the Royals might not be willing to go through it again. Better a team laced with locals, he figured, than a team loaded with tourists.

Mind you, he could afford to think that way. In those days, Canadian soccer was producing far more and far better players than the US variety. Local content wasn't a gimmick for us, it was a form of armament no other NASL side could match. Five of our opening-game starters—Ellett, Bruce Wilson, Glen Johnson, my brother Sam and myself were to be honoured, years later, by induction to the Canadian Soccer Association's Hall of Fame.

And then there was Brian Budd, a walking, talking media magnet and, for a new team struggling to get people's attention, a dream come true. How great an athlete was he? Consider this: Brian Budd didn't take up soccer until his late teens. By age twenty he was playing for the Whitecaps—and soccer was nowhere near his best sport. Brian was a fun guy who loved to party almost as much as he loved to tell stories, especially if they were on himself. During a game with the New York Cosmos, he said, Pelé himself paid him a huge compliment: "You're not the best player I've met," said the legend, "but you're the funniest." Brian had his own spin on that: "When you're noticed by Pelé," he'd chortle, "you must have *something*."

Pelé wasn't alone. In 1994, as Team Canada got ready for an exhibition match against Germany, coach Berti Vogts recalled playing an exhibition match against the Whitecaps. This is a man who'd played fifteen seasons for Borussia Mönchengladbach and twelve years on the German national side, but that one game stuck in his mind.

"You had this big blond player," he recalled. "He wasn't very skilful, but he ran over me several times."

Budd had something all right: incredible conditioning that allowed him to leave competitors gasping in his wake and the ability to pick up any sport and play it full throttle and well.

This did not escape the eye of the promotion-minded Capozzi, who was forever trumpeting that Budd was the best-conditioned athlete in Vancouver. He once bet—with much media fanfare, of course—that Budd could run up the stairs to the top of the new Sears Tower office building in less than three minutes, which he did.

"Piece of cake," Capozzi crowed. "He even beat the elevator to the top."

Brian was with the Whitecaps for our first four years, then bounced around the NASL a bit before finishing with the Toronto Blizzard, but his biggest claim to fame came in the televised US *Superstars* series competition, which he won for three straight years (1978–80) against some of world's top athletes in a series of competitions in various sports. He made it look so easy that the desperate producers finally concocted what came to be called "the Budd rule," stating that no competitor could win the event more than three times.

(I was in *Superstars* in 1977. I was terrible, but got to the semifinals of the tennis event, where I lost to Mike Bossy of the New York Islanders. I managed to do four chin-ups, but the judge said I hadn't locked my elbow and gave me a zero. By that time I was done and just hung there like an idiot. Budd, of course, could do them all day long.)

Strangely enough, Brian never truly won over our fans, who booed him mercilessly as he roared around the pitch at breakneck speed, making up in enthusiasm, athleticism and sheer determination what he lacked in skill. Nonetheless, he had his moments. Named to start against the Los Angeles Aztecs, he scored two goals, set up the other in a 3–1 victory and still found time to rush in with fists flying when he felt several of the Aztecs were roughing up a teammate.

He remained the guy our fans loved to boo, but a lot of it came to be more a sign of good-natured affection than of criticism. They even made a joke of the *Superstars* events, claiming he had an unfair advantage because you couldn't compete in the sport in which you made your living, so he didn't have to embarrass himself by entering the soccer event.

Wherever he played, though, his teammates loved the guy they called Budgie, who never lost his zeal for competing, whether it was on the pitch or at the party he and his three roomies—all athletes, all single—threw once a year in Toronto in the '80s.

"The first year there were about 200 guests," one of the regulars recalled. "The third year there were somewhere between 600 and 1,000. The neighbours called the police and shut it down."

Budgie stayed connected with soccer as one of the colour commentators on The Score network's telecasts of Premier League games. We lost him too soon, from an apparent heart attack in 2010, but as long as there are Whitecap stories there will be tales of Budgie. Wherever he is, he'll like that.

As for our import players, Easton struck gold by luring Liverpool veteran Billy Stevenson, whose resumé included more than 300 matches and an FA Cup Final player-of-the-game award. He was past his prime, but his legendary passing skills were still very much in evidence and, as Sam said, watching him play was like having an on-the-spot coaching clinic. Stevenson was our on-field leader.

George "Dandy" McLean, late of the Glasgow Rangers and the man who, in Easton's mind, figured to be our goal-scoring ace was, well, just Dandy. He was the funniest man I ever met—every time he opened his mouth you'd burst out laughing—and the man could score goals, or so it seemed at first. He scored all three of our goals on our first two-game road trip. Unfortunately, he got only two more throughout the entire season. But, man, could he keep us loose. Take a look at that opening-night lineup:

Our keeper was Sam "save-it-again-Sam" Nusum, who'd starred the previous season with the now-defunct Montreal franchise. Ellett, Wilson, Sam and I were on defence; Dandy, Johnson and Canadian Victor Kadelja were at forward; Brian Gant and Daryl Samson were in the midfield and Stevenson served as our link man. Les Wilson, only twenty-six but already with nine years in English football with Wolverhampton, Bristol City and Norwich, was en route and soon a regular. Our bench seemed solid—all in all, a team of great promise.

Unfortunately, it didn't happen. The goals didn't come. We out-shot everyone, but we just couldn't finish, and we positively sucked at the shootout. We finished last in our division, which was particularly frustrating because had we been in the Northern Division our 45 points would have been good for second place.

Still, that first season provided some great memories, not the least of which was playing in Empire Stadium with the mountains in the background giving us a venue unmatched, in scenic terms at least, by any in the league.

Okay, the field's artificial turf resembled green paint spread over asphalt, and anyone foolish enough to attempt a slide tackle, as years of instinct and training insisted that we did, would feel like he was leaving chunks of his arse in his wake. By halftime, bloodied buttocks were like part of the uniform. When it rained, the water just sat on top of the turf, sometimes so deep that if you had any momentum when you fell you turned bodysurfer and could slide for yards.

One thing about it, though: on artificial turf the bounce was always true, unlike matches on some of the English grass playing surfaces, which by mid-season were laced with ruts and ridges that sent the ball in every direction but the one you expected. On artificial turf, you knew what the ball was going to do when it hit. (Peter Beardsley, who was with us for three years in the early '80s and had a professional career lasting an incredible twenty seasons, always credited the Empire turf for giving him his early confidence.)

A crowd favourite from the day he arrived in 1981 as a twenty-year-old with a world of talent, Peter Beardsley had three seasons (and twenty-eight goals) with the Whitecaps, launching a pro career that spanned two decades and included fifty-nine caps for England. KENT KALLBERG

Anyway, we didn't make the playoffs, and in the off-season we ran into a curious backlash: our fans asked why they should be expected to pay to watch a team loaded with local players when they could skip the NASL's summer league, wait until BC soccer's regular fall and winter season and watch the same guys on their club teams for nothing.

Initially it was a two-pronged criticism: the local player issue and the fact that fans from the various ethnic groups—whose memories of home were so rose-tinted they refused to admit that they'd *ever* seen a game in their native land that was anything less than great—were forever complaining that our roster didn't have enough players from (insert country). Easton, with no budget to speak of, could do nothing about that aspect, but now those same fans were complaining about the BC-bred content?

Denny and Herb realized something had to be done, so Denny called in the local players and expressed his sympathy, but said if they wanted to stay with the Whitecaps they'd have to stop playing with their club teams in our off-season—which was fair enough, I suppose, until you broke it down.

The local players, who made up about 90 percent of the roster, were playing for next to no money, in most cases $500 a month with some getting only $125. That meant getting an outside job to make ends meet and, for many, making sacrifices in terms of what was going to be their life's work when their soccer careers ended so that they *could* play this game that they loved.

Bruce Wilson, for example, had a teaching job waiting when he joined the team in 1974 after graduating from University of BC, but the school board looked at the travel and the potential complications and told him that if he wanted the job he had to make a choice: teaching or soccer. Bruce thought it over and chose soccer. Greg Weber's future was in dentistry, but there he was, playing in goal without any insurance when broken fingers could make handling the tools of his trade a problem for him, never mind what it would do to his customers' confidence. And did I mention that when the team went on the road and guys had to miss work to make the trip there was no compensation for lost wages?

For me, of course, the game was Reading-Vancouver-Reading, one year-long and happy season and easy enough when you're young. I raise the issue only to show the dedication and commitment of the Canadian players. When Veitch gave them the bad news, the players with no winter pro or semi-pro connections *agreed with him* and informed their local teams that they wouldn't be rejoining them. What's more, the day after the Whitecaps' season ended, a bunch of them got together for regular training sessions through the winter because they *wouldn't* be playing and wanted to stay in shape so they'd be ready when the Whitecaps opened camp for the next season.

I think of that sometimes when I read of millionaire players in other sports whining because they're unappreciated and so underpaid they can barely afford to buy that second or third Maserati or put the full-sized basketball court and the indoor pool in their mansions. How would their love of their games stand up against our guys' love for theirs?

Easton, who often said his only problem with our Canadian players was convincing them that they belonged and collectively were as good or better than any club in the NASL, had an interesting answer in his second season to fans who weren't happy with our Canadian content. He increased it, replacing Nusum with national team goalie Peter Greco, declining to invite Dandy McLean back, and adding Bruce Twamley and Sergio Zanatta, who'd each sat out the '74 season with a broken leg.

Unfortunately, the fans still weren't buying it. Either that, or maybe Capozzi and Veitch and their financial partners had guessed wrong and the marketplace just wasn't ready to support professional soccer. We had to wonder. We opened at home with three victories. The first one drew 10,000 fans who saw us play a wide-open, entertaining game, winning 1–0 over Chicago Sting. Apparently, that wasn't good enough. Five days later we beat Seattle 2–1 and the crowd had dropped to 7,500, which was 264 more than came to see us whip Toronto 4–1.

So, there we were—undefeated, but beginning to suspect that not many cared, because when we came back from our first road trip unbeaten in five, our home game against Portland drew the same faithful 7,000-plus. They saw us lose 2–0 and probably went home complaining that we were using too many Canadians.

It was hard to figure. We were in contention for first place in our division and no one seemed to care. In San Jose they were routinely drawing 18,000. Portland and Seattle had good crowds and a rabid fan base, some of whom even made trips. It was an attitudinal thing. You want to know the difference? In San Jose the Earthquakes had a soon-to-be-famous cheerleader named Krazy George who lifted the crowd into a frenzy whenever they scored. In Vancouver we had a horse named Pride who raced around the stadium track whenever we scored. Nobody seemed to care—except when we *didn't* score, and then people joked that the poor horse spent the entire game just standing there and at the current rate might forget *how* to run.

Capozzi was doing everything he could, even offering fans a money-back guarantee if they weren't entertained by a home game against the Earthquakes. We lost 3–2 in overtime in a wildly entertaining match—and thirty fans demanded their money back. He brought in a cheerleader to do what Krazy George was doing in San Jose—and our fans booed him every time he tried to lead a cheer.

We stumbled through the rest of the season. Maybe it was discouragement, I don't know, but we didn't make the playoffs, and Jim Easton was fired in the off-season. "You know the difference between the Whitecaps and the big US NASL teams?" he asked in his final press conference. "We tried to build a team. They went out and bought one."

Certainly he had a point in the case of the New York Cosmos, who were averaging fewer than 5,000 fans per game until Warner Brothers took a bunch of their movie money and did the unthinkable. They lured the world's most famous player out of retirement.

Edson Arantes do Nascimento, better known as Pelé, joined the Cosmos in the middle of the '75 season for a salary listed as a minimum $4 million and guesstimated as high as $7 million. In star-struck New York, the effect was instantaneous. At the press conference that made the signing official, fist fights broke out between the reporters and the TV and radio guys as they battled for clear camera sight lines or seats in the front row so they could scribble his every word. With one signing, the Cosmos had given the struggling NASL instant credibility. It came with a price: Warners and the Cosmos setting world records for arrogance, acting as though they ran the league—and sometimes it seemed that they did. Consider this: when the Pelé signing was just a rumour, we went into New York and beat the Cosmos 1–0 before only 7,331 fans. Every Cosmos' home game from then on drew a sellout 23,000. Home or road, Pelé was king. The point had been made: sport was entertainment, and entertainment meant star power.

In theory, then, what we needed was a big-name star of our own and a coach who leaned toward wide-open, entertaining soccer that would allow us to showcase that star's talents and draw people into the park.

We went 0-for-2. The big name was never signed and our coach was Eckhard Krautzun, whose idea of a perfect game plan was to score the first goal, then turn out the lights, pack our defence and hope the other team couldn't find our net in the dark.

Krautzun's credentials were indisputable. A former star with 1FC Kaiserslautern in Germany's first division, he'd gone directly into coaching and, at age thirty-five, his resumé already showed a successful stint with Zurich in Switzerland's first division and with national teams in Korea, Kenya and Japan, guiding the Japanese to the bronze medal at the 1972 Olympic Games in Munich. One problem: there should have been an asterisk next to his name at the top as in *quirky.

What Capozzi had gone looking for was a coach whose international credentials would be recognized and respected by those dyed-in-the-wool soccer fans we couldn't seem to attract, someone who could rightly be trumpeted as world class. Unfortunately, Herb's scouting report on Krautzun didn't mention his coaching paranoia or his press conference penchant for opening mouth and inserting foot. Nor did it note that when the Good Lord passed out the senses of humour, Eckhard must have been on a coffee break. Players were always making jokes at his expense, and he never understood.

It must have been a strange situation for him. Since Canada had no real national team program and much of our roster was Canadian, we weren't just the Whitecaps. We were, in effect, the national side. When international competitions surfaced, we'd drop our imports and go. And the coach of that team was *also* Eckhard Krautzun, so we had a two-tier view of the quirkiness.

Quirky? Well, let's see . . .

He'd pay random visits to players' residences and check the fridge to see if they were eating properly. When the national team went to other countries, he'd tell us to check under our hotel room beds for listening devices. None of us ever did, but he truly believed they might be there.

In the first CONCACAF qualifying series in the run-up to the World Cup, when we were getting ready for a home game against Mexico (which we won 1–0 on a goal by Buzz Parsons), Eckhard saw a maintenance guy sweeping out the Empire Stadium stands during practice and raced up the steps to confront him and demand that he leave. Why? Because he might be spying for the Mexicans.

I'm not trying to slag Eckhard. He fought to make the White-caps a better side, and he did. Unfortunately, most of those fights were with management, and he was never shy about launching his missiles during media conferences.

He'd been given a budget increase that allowed him to lure a handful of Brits (including goalie Phil "Lofty" Parkes, who was destined to play such a vital role for us down the road), but for Krautzun it was nowhere near enough, and he didn't hesitate to say so. At one memorable media conference he dismissed the team's organization as not even semi-professional, announced that with a goalie, a midfielder and a first-rate striker the team might be good enough to go all the way, and then added that getting them would cost $500,000, which happened to be ten times Easton's budget the previous year.

The guy just never knew when to shut up. Yes, our crowds were down to the point where media speculation and a warning from Capozzi that things had to improve triggered speculation that we'd be gone at the end of the year, but we were winning. After five games we led the entire NASL. So what did Eckhard do after that fifth game? He told the media to be sure to get what he was about to say because he wanted it known that if the team didn't get him a mid-fielder very soon, "I will personally take action to do so. If management doesn't take action to get this player, *I* will."

Really? How was he going to do that? Pay the guy's salary out of his own pocket?

And then there was the night that, in Krautzun's mind at least, sex reared its ugly head. We'd been stumbling a bit and, two days after a 3–0 drubbing by the Minnesota Kicks, he attributed the slump to the fact that that several players "were involved in such poisonous things as sex." Media types must have chortled as he rapped several of his "immature" players who lacked a professional approach to the game.

"Too much sex can drain you," he was quoted as saying. "Sex can be a dangerous thing in soccer. You take a bachelor on our team. If he exercises three or four times before a game he is tired. He has nothing left for the match." Reporters were left to speculate on what he meant by "exercises." There was no shortage of definitions.

We made the playoffs, finishing third in our division, and got ready to face the Seattle Sounders, sudden death, in the concrete bunker that was the Kingdome. We out-shot them convincingly but still lost 1–0, for which Krautzun had a curious explanation: "They completely upset our plan by scoring the first goal," he told the *Vancouver Sun*. "It was *our* plan to score first." Once again, he went semi-postal on the people who were paying his salary, dismissing the team's management level as amateurish and warning that unless things changed, he wouldn't be back.

However, he couldn't leave yet. Reluctantly, he had to don his national team hat for the CONCACAF playoffs, which was kind of funny in a way because, with Labatt's kicking in $100,000, the Whitecaps—the team he was threatening to leave—were now the official national team sponsor.

We won four, drew four and lost three, failed to advance, and went home to re-don our Whitecaps mentalities while we waited to see who won the management vs. Krautzun showdown that the players now considered inevitable. Something had to happen and something did: a man named John Best.

5

PROMISES, PROMISES

"The name of the game is identity, and without it, teams die young."
—*Vancouver Sun*, May 1978

If Herb Capozzi knew one thing as he looked ahead to our fourth NASL season it was that we were in need of an image overhaul. The fans weren't buying Krautzun's score-and-bar-the-door coaching philosophy, and the media weren't buying Krautzun.

In a way, that last part was a shame. Eckhard was a good coach who believed that his duties began and ended with that coaching, and nothing or no one should be allowed to get in the way. With an established team in an established market, that can work and often does. In a market with a skeptical and scanty fan base, the media play a vital role in the matter of whether customer thumbs go up or down. And unless he was using them as megaphones to trumpet his management criticisms, Eckhard viewed the media the way kids view castor oil.

Capozzi knew that the fix would require more than a band-aid and the same old promises. It might take a miracle man, a media-friendly, customer-friendly guy, smooth enough to woo fans old and new without sounding like a used-car salesman. He'd also have to be soundly rooted and knowledgeable enough in the game to find and sign the type of players who would fit into the open, entertaining style that would get butts in seats for a look and convince them to come back. So, in the off-season, he reached out and found one.

It must have been a tough decision, because bringing in a new general manager meant removing the old one. Denny Veitch was a good friend who'd been there from the beginning, and if you looked in the dictionary under "dedication" or "commitment" you'd probably find his picture. Come to think of it, you might also find it under "intimidating," which you might not expect, given his physical presence.

At age six, Denny lost his right arm at the shoulder under a train wheel as he tried to jump from a boxcar onto which he and his brother had scrambled as they played at the train tracks that ran near their home. Logic says that should have taken him out of contact sports. Not Denny. The loss only made him that much more determined not only to play, but to excel. He stayed with his first love, rugby, and not only competed but made a name as a fierce, no-quarter tackler who played for Canada in international competition and became something of a legend, particularly in Japan with its large disabled community.

The tackling skills alone would have given him a shot at linebacker in junior football, but for Denny that apparently wasn't enough of a challenge. He made the team as a receiver, running his routes, batting balls out of the air and gathering them into

Denny Veitch—a great athlete in his own right, the Whitecaps' first general manager, the guy who signed me and, oh, yes, my father-in-law—does some grandpa time with our daughter, Sunny. LENARDUZZI COLLECTION

his chest. (In later years he'd also joke of his fishing prowess, holding out his arm, eyeing the spot where the other one might have been, and crowing that "I caught one *this long*.")

It wasn't that Denny didn't accept his injury; he simply refused to let it make any difference. Muscular through the chest, he played racquetball (I think I still have welts on my ass from playing him, because if you got in his way you were going down) and stayed exceptionally fit. He'd come to work in shirt and tie, the empty sleeve neatly pinned to the jacket. Unless you're in the Boy Scouts, hand-shaking is done with the right, so he would turn his hand to keep it that way rather than have people awkwardly sticking out their left.

When he made his pitch in 1973 to get me to the Whitecaps the following summer it wasn't based on personal assessment. He knew little if anything about soccer, only that I was Canadian and playing in England and that therefore I must be pretty good. But, know the game or not, he was a rules-are-rules guy, which led to a situation worthy of a television sitcom.

The Whitecaps had a group of young women who'd be sent out to represent the club at various functions and our home games, all part of the plan to keep the club in the public eye. The group included Denny's two daughters, Deanne and Karen, and if the players knew one thing it was that the girls were so off-limits they might as well be on another planet. On the other hand, we were young, they were young, boys will be boys, and Deanne and Karen were really good looking. Sooo . . .

I met Deanne at a team party put on by one of the directors in 1974, the same gathering at which Daryl Samson met Karen. The problem was, neither had mentioned their *last* name. When the party ended, Daryl drove Karen home. They're sitting in her living room with her mother, Iris, when Daryl hears a car come up the driveway. The front door opens—and there stands Denny, staring at this *player* who has apparently been out with his high-school-age daughter. Daryl's whole life flashes before his eyes. Visions of unemployment dance through his head, and he sets a world speed record for goodbye and exit.

The thing was he really *liked* Karen, and he began dating her, all unbeknownst to Denny. They, in turn, set me up with Deanne. Fortunately, Iris liked us, encouraged the outings and said nothing to her husband. Life went on, Deanne and I enjoying a few casual dates, Daryl and Karen were clearly falling in love and were destined to marry. Me? I went to Reading.

We corresponded, but when I came home in '76 she wasn't even in town. I was in the dating game, of course—nothing serious—but one night at a club three years later, Karen told me there was someone who wanted to say hello. And there she was.

You'll have to excuse me now, because things get hokey. I am the worst dancer, but we're in a club and out on the floor, me and this girl I used to know. The second dance is a slow one, and I ask her if she's listening to the words. The song is "Reunited" by Peaches and Herb. We'd dated, gone our separate ways, and now we were—wait for it—reunited. Okay, go ahead: gag.

We knew we had something special. It had to be, because our wedding date in the fall of '81 was postponed a couple of times due to my soccer commitments, and when we finally settled on November 28, I was absent for the five weeks leading up to it because of qualification matches in Honduras. It was an indicator of how our life was going to be, and of how supportive and understanding of that fact Deanne could be. Okay, we didn't qualify for the World Cup, but I won something far better.

Family gatherings were interesting, Daryl and I suggesting to Denny that, since we were part of the family now, maybe the GM could find it in his heart to give his sons-in-law more money ("You were lousy negotiators," Denny would later shoot back. "Was that *my* fault?"). All was well, but I bet it took a while for Daryl to get his heart out of his throat.

Oh, by the way, do you know what we chose for our wedding song? Peaches and Herb doing "Reunited." Who says romance is dead?

There was another factor in Denny's move away from the Whitecaps. Iris had been diagnosed with cancer, which would prove to be

To put it in sports terms, Deanne was my first draft choice, my greatest signing and the biggest bonus I ever received. The contract, naturally, was a lifetime deal. LENARDUZZI COLLECTION

terminal, and he wanted to spend as much time as possible with her. In soccer terms, the move was a logical step for a team battling to get established in the local market. For all his devotion to the task at hand, Denny was a Canadian football man who'd come into soccer as a neophyte and tried to learn on the job. John Best, Capozzi's choice to succeed him, was soccer-bred-and-born—seventeen years as a player in England, five times an NASL all-star defender, successful head coach of the Seattle Sounders in their first three years.

He was smart, he was smooth, and he could charm a dog off a pork chop. More than that, he was a born salesman who'd gone out into the community in Seattle and played a large part in building the new team's fan base into one of the league's best. Plus, the Seattle media loved him. If the same charm worked in Vancouver . . .

Mind you, with Krautzun back as coach, that wasn't going to

be easy. Clearly the off-season hadn't been long enough to warm his relationship with the people covering his team.

The NASL had a rule stipulating that the media had to be allowed in the dressing room no later than fifteen minutes after a game. Eckhard grandly announced that he had overruled that rule. When he finally swung open the door after the next game, there was no one there. The media—led by Jim Taylor, then the *Sun*'s front sports page columnist—boycotted the post-game, did their work in the press box and went home.

Maybe Eckhard didn't get the message, but Best did. He arranged a Krautzun-media press conference and even provided two sets of boxing gloves, suggesting that Krautzun and Taylor don them for a photo op. He had no takers. Eckhard—surprise!—couldn't see the humour and Taylor said the boycott had been to make a point. As long as the dressing room was opened on schedule, no problem.

I'm not sure how long Best and Krautzun could have worked together. Their philosophies weren't designed to co-exist. At his first press conference, Best laid out his platform, based on a firm belief that, ideally, the city loves the team, the team loves the city, and everyone from directors and general manager to coach and players had to do his or her part to win over the soccer public, to prove that affection was genuine by going out into the community and getting involved. Eckhard, on the other hand, believed his job was to coach, period. Oh, and screw entertaining the customers. Only the result counted.

Tic-tic-tic-tic . . .

Things came to a head three days after a 3–0 shootout victory over Dallas in front of 8,471 dozing Empire Stadium fans. Out of the blue, Krautzun announced that he was leaving. Officially, he said it was because (a) he needed to devote all his efforts to the national team (curious, in that he'd never shown much indication that he'd ever wanted that job in the first place) and (b) he needed to go back to Germany to take a mandatory refresher course to maintain his coaching licence there and the Whitecaps wouldn't give him a leave of absence to do so.

Well, maybe. More likely, he knew his Whitecap days would end at season's close and he preferred to leave on his own terms without a firing on his resumé. Whatever. Eckhard was a fine coach who'd given it his best effort in a marketplace that needed, if we were to survive as a franchise, an approach that was foreign to his very nature. Love him or hate him, no one could fault his work ethic.

Best went looking for a new coach whose philosophy matched his own. We went on a three-game road trip with Holger Osieck as reluctant playing head coach, and lost all three. By the time we got home, Best had his man in place, sitting in the stands among the 7,241 watching us beat Ft. Lauderdale 2–1. His name was Tony Waiters . . .

Tony likes to say that the Whitecaps' offer was a perfect fit. ("Krautzun had been fired in Vancouver and I'd just been fired in Plymouth.") But

On the inside, his stomach might be churning, but on the outside, no matter how tense the situation, Tony Waiters was ever calm and imperturbable. From the moment they took over, he and GM John Best were the architects of our success. KENT KALLBERG

that doesn't quite tell it. A former FA goalkeeper with 250-plus appearances for Blackpool and 40 more with Burnley, he'd led Plymouth to the third division championship and promotion in 1975. The firing two years later meant little. Everyone knows that managers are hired to be fired. Best knew that their approaches to the game would mesh and that Tony's affability would buy him the time he might need to adjust to the quirks of the skeptical Vancouver media. Other than employment, the lure for Tony was a fascination with the goings-on in the NASL. He couldn't see himself settling long-term in North America (as, of course, he did), but a short-term job-cum-holiday was appealing. The contract he signed was for three or four months until the end of the season. After that, he could decide. Meanwhile, there was the challenge of rebuilding a franchise.

He didn't waste any time. Almost before the fans could blink they were looking at 5'6" Gordon Taylor and 5'5" Derek Possee. With ex-Chelsea midfielder Brian Bason and Tommy Ord, obtained in trade from Toronto in mid-1976, that gave us four starters 5'8" or under, prompting media suggestions that the team was rebuilding from the ground up, but not very far up. Waiters couldn't have cared less. In his first game at the helm he started all of them in a four-man, all-British forward line, pushed our back four up to be more involved in the attack, and we beat the Connecticut Bicentennials 2–1.

Certainly we didn't feel small. Well, okay, sometimes, after our workouts at Empire Stadium, which we shared with the CFL's BC Lions. We'd be coming off as they were coming on. Someone really should have gotten a picture: us in our shorts, the Lions in their full shoulder pads, some of them closer to seven feet tall than to six, looking down at us as we passed. Of course, *we* knew that we were just as much athletes as they were. Somehow I doubt they shared the belief, particularly the American imports, who looked like they were waiting for us to pull out scraps of paper and ask for autographs.

Naturally there were complaints that we had too many Englishmen—most of them, I suspected, not from people among the 6,992 faithful who showed up to watch the win over Connecticut but from die-hard old-schoolers who preferred to stay home where they could bitch.

The criticism made no sense on several counts. First, Waiters' background and connections were in the English leagues. Second, those connections enabled him to know who might come available, and actually sign them at better than reasonable cost. He *knew* the style and character of the players he was bringing in. He'd seen them play. Heck, he'd seen *me* play with the Reading reserves and had decided even before he got to Vancouver that I could be a key part of the rebuilding process—even if, at his first press conference, he called me "Lenar-DOOCHIE."

As Jim Easton had in our first two seasons, Waiters saw the Canadian talent pool as an asset. A good thing, too, because Best had added to it with the likes of Gary Ayre, Bob Bolitho, Dale Mitchell (just eighteen but ready to take his first professional step on the road to the CSA Hall of Fame) and Buzz Parsons.

Parsons was a national team member who'd initially rejected Krautzun's persistent requests that he turn pro in '76, but he changed his mind after one of those bizarre screw-ups that always seemed to plague the national program. Buzzy had broken his leg in a national team game against Haiti in 1973, but was back on the squad over the next two years as well as playing for Simon Fraser University. The dream was intact: to make a spot on the Olympic team in 1976. The westerners on the national team had a regular conditioning program at SFU in the off-season that year—not a camp, just a regular gathering to stay in top shape.

On the day of one session, Buzzy's father-in-law produced two tickets for the NHL game between the Canucks and (Omigod!) the *Montreal Canadiens.* Would Buzz like to use them? That afternoon he put a note on the blackboard at SFU explaining that he'd be missing that night's workout because he had hockey tickets.

The next night, during a national team exhibition game, he was handed a piece of paper. Assuming it was the form the team wanted all the players to sign saying they'd stay amateur until after the Olympics, he stuffed it in his pocket and didn't read it until he got home.

It wasn't the form. It was a note saying he'd been cut from the national roster. Skipping that workout to watch the Canucks meet the Canadiens apparently marked him as a softie and brought his commitment into question.

He could have fought it, but to what purpose? How much would he play after bucking the brass? "Screw it," he thought, and signed with the Whitecaps. We were delighted, but it did raise questions about who, if anyone, was running the national program, and how they must have felt on that night later in the season when Buzzy became the first Whitecap ever to record a hat trick—and against Germany's touring Borussia Mönchengladbach at that—as we beat them 4–3.

The Olympic team didn't get past the first round, losing both its games and scoring only two goals. Would Buzz have made a difference? We'll never know.

There are games you remember for the excitement, the superstars or the dazzling play. Our seventeenth game in that 1977 season, against the New York Cosmos, had all those ingredients, but I remember it for another reason: to me, it was one of the pivotal games in Whitecaps' history.

The Cosmos had Pelé making what amounted to his farewell tour as a player, Franz Beckenbauer, Germany's legendary Kaiser Franz, had just signed, and then there was the veteran Georgio Chinaglia. They called him the Slot Machine, as Phil Esposito was called in hockey, and for the same reason: he seemed to take root in front of the opposition net. He also thought marking was a job for schoolteachers—but get him the ball and it was in.

Things were starting to turn for us. New players, a new system and the Best-Waiters unfailing faith (publicly, at least) were paying dividends. We were contenders with a legitimate shot at the league title, but the crowds were merely inching toward respectability, and we'd just taken a 5–2 drubbing in Chicago. If we took another one from the Cosmos in front of what we knew would be our biggest crowd of the season, the rest of the home games might not draw enough to fill bridge tables.

When we went out for the warm-up we were greeted by this strange noise—strange to us, at least. There were 30,277 people packed into Empire Stadium, and they were roaring their throats raw. Finally, we could show the local soccer community what it had been missing—and we did. Buzzy and Derek each scored twice, the game was wide open and wildly exciting, and we beat them 5–3. "If they didn't like that," Bruce Wilson huffed as we left the pitch, "we'd better get this team the hell out of town."

The post-game question, of course, was "How many people only came to see Pelé, and how many will come back to see us when we play Seattle on Tuesday?" The answer was a satisfying 14,559, and a lot of them must have made up their minds at the last moment. So many fans jammed the wickets in the ninety minutes before kickoff that they couldn't all be handled and at least 1,500 gave up and went home. But we had turned an important corner. The fans were out there. It was our job to maintain a level of play that would keep them interested. We did just that and finished second in our division to set up a home playoff game against the Sounders that drew 18,037.

The result was a crushing 2–0 defeat, and another game of second-guess.

With eight games left in the regular season, midfielder Horst Koeppel came back into the lineup, which would have meant benching Tommy Ord when both men had earned the right to start and neither would have been happy sitting on the sidelines. John Best solved the problem by trading Ord to Seattle, and Tommy did not take it well. Before the playoff game he told reporters it would be a delight to score and shove the trade up our arse, which is just what he did, scoring once and setting up the other goal.

It made for much what-if media commentary, but that's the way it goes with trades. Sometimes they come back to bite you. To us, the discussion was meaningless. The season was over, and don't give me that stuff about looking on the bright side at the progress we'd made. Losing has no bright side, and you don't just shift into "we'll-get-'em-next-year." That takes time. It would come—but not yet.

6

SOFA, SO GOOD

"Gordon Taylor??? Hell, I'm *better than him!"*
—Alan Hinton, 1978

When John and Tony began to rebuild and reshape the Whitecaps franchise they put the emphasis on character, singular, not characters, plural, but that didn't mean we didn't have our share of talent that marched to a different drum or, in one case, a different bagpipe.

Let me introduce you to some of them.

We got Willie Johnston because he'd blown a drug test after Scotland's first game of the 1978 World Cup and was banned forever from that competition and for one year from plying his trade in Europe. Willie's plea that he'd taken a cold tablet called Reactivan and was unaware that it contained something on FIFA's ever-changing and expanding list of prohibited drugs was ignored, although there was historical precedent. In 1976, organizers for the Montreal Olympic Games put up billboards trumpeting another brand as "the official cold tablet of the Olympic Games" and had to tear them down when someone noticed that the tablet contained one of the banned drugs on the International Olympic Committee list.

So I believed Willie and still do. Lord knows, his misfortune was our gain. As for Willie, all he wanted to do was put the whole mess behind him. Still, he must have wondered what he'd gotten himself into when Tony joked during his introduction at a press conference that one of the inducements he'd used to get him was to remind Willie that Vancouver was the drug capital of Canada.

Willie quickly showed us what a great deal it was going to be. At thirty-three he'd lost a step from the days when he scored twice for the Glasgow Rangers in the European Cup Winners Cup Final in 1972 and was purchased by West Bromwich Albion for a club record £138,000, but roaming the wing with the ball on his boot he could still tie opponents in knots. For Willie, one-on-one was a joke.

It made playing with him an experience. He'd always be asking for the ball and seemed happiest when he had two or three defenders around him. Time and time again I'd give it to him, race past him on the overlap, and never get it back. To Willie, I was almost always the decoy.

Now, those overlaps mean long runs from the back. I'd be gasping and to no avail, because I was never getting the ball. Finally, moving to get back into position, I put it to him:

"Willie, c'mon. Why don't you *ever* play it back to me?"

I expected some technical explanation or excuse. Not Willie.

"Because," he deadpanned, "I don't *like* you."

All I could do was laugh.

For all his talent, it was his showmanship that won over the paying customers and drew them to Empire Stadium in increasing numbers, which we found rather strange considering his off-field lifestyle. That was so quiet that the *Vancouver Sun* reported, after a fruitless search for evidence that the private Willie was at least a little bit as flamboyant as the one in football boots, "If all the Scots were as quiet as the public Willie, the national drink would be embalming fluid." First and foremost, Willie was show biz.

"If a man works hard all week, spends his money and brings his kids to the match, he's got a right to be entertained," he said. "Win

When he was one-on-one with anybody, in open field or in a phone booth, no one who'd seen him in action would ever bet against Willie Johnston. KENT KALLBERG

We had him only for the 1978 season, but Alan Hinton put on a magic show, setting up headers with crosses and set pieces so accurate he could pick which eyebrow he wanted to hit. I was on the receiving end for a lot of them. JOHN DENNISTON

or lose, they should be able to go home saying they *enjoyed* themselves. That's why I do what I do."

With the possible exception of the time he scored a goal and mooned the opposition bench, Willie's most famous Whitecap escapade came on a night in San Jose as he lined up a corner kick. The stands were only a couple of feet away and it was a hot night, so when a fan leaned over and offered him a beer, how could he resist? He took the proffered bottle, had a swig, set it on the ledge—and swung in the corner that set up Peter Daniel's winning goal.

It made headlines all over the NASL, such as "When Willie Saw the Lite!" What people didn't realize was that this was a rerun. At West Brom he once preceded a corner kick by buying a greenhouse from a fan. The guy was a regular who knew Willie was an avid gardener. Willie's greenhouse was back home in Scotland and the fan had one for sale. Negotiations went on for several home games, and Willie finally closed the deal as he was putting the ball down for a corner kick, which was great. "So was the price," he said. For Willie, that explained everything.

Oh, and about that mooning incident when we were playing the exhibition against Scotland. He wasn't mooning club or country. He was mooning Bruce Rioch, the Scottish captain with whom he'd played in his brief World Cup appearance the year before—and he had his reasons.

As Willie told it, prior to the World Cup the Scottish players had decided to pool all the money any of them made for appearances and suchlike and divide it equally through the whole squad at the end. Rioch, however, had apparently done some things independently and pocketed the money. To Willie, that was breaking ranks. Hence, the moon. With Willie, there was always method to his madness, and what a joy he was.

And then there was Roger Kenyon, who had no trouble keeping a positive attitude despite a string of niggling injuries. When you've had your throat cut twice and had a blanket put over you while ambulance attendants readied the body bag because they thought you were dead, something as simple as a hamstring injury is barely worth mentioning.

In 1977 he was in the passenger seat of a car that hit a pole. Roger went though the windshield, leaving much of his throat on the glass. You could excuse the ambulance guys for thinking he was a goner. His face had chunks of glass embedded in it. His throat was one gaping slash. Fortunately, one of them thought he detected a faint pulse. They raced him to hospital, he was rushed into surgery and after massive transfusions doctors deemed the crisis over. That one, anyway.

Stitching his throat back together left what looked like a sac around the neck area, swollen and full of blood. He was recuperating at home when he coughed. A shard of glass they'd missed came through the sac wall, slicing a vein en route. He grabbed a towel to jam against the wound and managed a yell to his wife, who called an ambulance. Had there not been a hospital nearby, there might have been another body bag. More surgery, more transfusions, another survival. Before the season was out he was back with Everton, the club for which he'd played since he was fifteen. Now he was a Whitecap hailed by Best as "the best central defender in the NASL."

"He's doing well now with the hamstring," Best concluded. "But I still worry every time he shaves."

Alan Hinton wasn't supposed to play at all. Waiters brought him in as an assistant coach in 1978, a winger of impeccable credentials—England under-23, top scorer with Wolverhampton in 1963, all-England that year and the next two, two years with Notts Forest, league first division championship in 1971–2 with Derby County where he enjoyed legendary success capped by a testimonial game in 1976.

Time and logic had put those skills in the past tense until Waiters mentioned that he was trying to sign Gordon Taylor (now the head of the Professional Footballers Association in England), who'd been a Whitecap in 1977 before returning to Blackburn Rovers, to strengthen a roster dangerously thinned by injuries.

"Hell," said Hinton, "I'm better than him."

"Well," Tony replied, "you'd better get rid of some weight and get into shape if you're planning on proving it."

His start was not promising. He was thirty-five, and far from match fit because he'd never expected to play. When he ran out onto the field the belly and butt jiggled, as one *Vancouver Province* columnist put it, "like two cats in a sack." But as the belly shrank and the legs remembered what they'd been, it started to come together. Set pieces or crosses, he could launch a ball 35 yards and drop it on a dime. "When Alan Hinton put a corner kick on your head," the *Sun* reported as the season wound down, "he'd give you your choice of eyebrows."

The NASL record for assists (a statistic initiated because American hockey fans might identify with it) was 18, shared by people named George Best and Pelé. There were 32,752 people in the Empire Stadium stands the night he tied that record with a 20-yard free kick lofted high into the box, where Robbie Campbell nodded it home. By season's end he hadn't just beaten the record, he'd obliterated it, finishing with an incredible 30.

Vancouver had a new darling. Then, just like that, he was gone, moving on to become head coach of the Tulsa Roughnecks. "Everything came together last year," he explained. "It was magic, but it wasn't going to happen twice. It was a good way to be remembered."

Amen.

Robbie Campbell spent only the last half of the 1978 season with us, a 6'1", 190-pound raw-boned Irishman who played up front and had a tendency to clear defenders like a tenpin ball hitting the headpin. But we loved him, and nobody could ever say he didn't leave his mark on the field, on the recording of our fight song or beside my mother's sofa.

Let's take the song first. It was John Best's idea, I suspect: take the Chelsea fight song, "Blue is the Colour," change "blue" to "white," send some of the team into a recording studio and make a record that might get some radio play and some free publicity. It was a brilliant idea, and it worked. His only mistake was putting Hinton in charge of getting the lads to the studio.

Hinton figured the boys might sing better if they were, well, loose. His way of loosening them was to troop them all to a local club called the No. 5 Orange for a beer. Okay, for a lot of beer. By the time they lined up to cut the record they were so loose it's a wonder parts didn't fall off.

Some outsiders with trained voices were added to the mix, Hinton had been a choir boy (picture that!) and some of the guys weren't too terrible, so away they went:

> *"White is the colour, soccer is the game,*
> *We're all together, and winning is our aim.*
> *So cheer us on through the sun and rain,*
> *For Whitecaps, Whitecaps is our name!*
> *Come to the park and we'll welcome you,*
> *Wear our white, see us through.*
> *Sing loud and clear till the day is done,*
> *Sing Whitecaps everyone!"*

It took more than a few run-throughs, but they finally had one they thought was pretty good. Then they played back the dub and discovered that Campbell, apparently caught up in the moment, had ended each sentence with "*You bleepers!*" Except that he didn't say "*bleepers*." What he said was—how should I put it? You know those First World War German fighter planes, the kind the Red Baron flew? Fokkers? Close enough.

Engineers had to go back, erase the sentence-ending comments, and re-dub. It all turned out well. The record received great radio play and sold an estimated ten thousand copies. It's lucky the screw-up on the original was caught, or we *really* would have gotten some media attention.

The sofa incident occurred because my mom decided it would be a nice thing to invite the whole team over to the house for dinner. In any Italian household, dinner means pasta, ravioli, spaghetti, the whole deal.

The team arrived, dinner was served and things seemed to be going really well. What we didn't know was that Campbell, your basic meat-and-potatoes Irishman, couldn't stand pasta.

I guess he didn't want to be rude. Rather than *say* he didn't like pasta, he accepted his heaping plate, sat down on the sofa and, bit by bit, slid the food off the plate and hid it behind the stereo speakers next to the sofa.

The next day, Hinton got a call from Waiters. "We've got a problem," he said, which was an understatement. My mom had found the hidden pasta.

Tony insisted that Hinton take Campbell over to the house to apologize, even though that was the last thing Mom wanted. They arrived, Bobby gave his apology and they turned to leave, but then Bobby had a thought.

"I'm missin' me favourite soap," he told her. "It's on right now. Can I watch it here?"

Mom didn't know what to say. Taking silence for permission, Bobby sat down on the same sofa, watched his soap, said goodbye and left. They don't make them like that any more.

The team didn't come together overnight. It took two seasons, and don't let the emphasis on character or all this stuff about fun and games and oddballs give you the wrong idea. Yes, we had our off-the-wall guys, but we also had toughness and a singleness of purpose. More than once, I found myself thinking "Jeez, I'd hate to be going *against* these guys!" We weren't flashy—in terms of skill level, teams like the Cosmos were better than us, hands down—but the flash guys didn't like playing us. Tony and John had put together a side in which everyone knew his role and understood that victory would come only through total team effort. You came to work every day and you did your job to the best of your ability. Our team logo should have been a black lunch box.

Oh, and one other thing the flash guys knew: the Whitecaps took no prisoners.

We weren't a dirty side, but you played us at your peril, particularly in 1979, because every time you looked up you saw Kenyon, the bearded, physical, mean-looking bad-ass anchoring the middle. And next to him, usually with a quizzical half-smile on his face, was the human stop sign called Cravo.

John Craven came to us in 1978 after a dozen years in England with Blackpool, Crystal Palace, Coventry City and Plymouth Argyle. He was tough, he was motivated, and he neither gave nor asked for any quarter. Four games into his career as a Whitecap he had a nickname, courtesy of Jim Taylor in the *Vancouver Sun*, who pinned him perfectly as "The Elegant Thug."

Maybe the best way to explain Cravo is to recall him in action. It's 1979, we're playing the Cosmos, and Willie and their Iranian fullback Andranik Eskandarian are having their own private war. They'd faced each other in the World Cup the year before and there was no love lost between them. Now they were at it again, and it reached the point where you wondered why they bothered with the ball at all, because neither guy seemed too concerned with it as they hacked and punched and finally wound up in a brawling heap on the turf.

Well, that was okay—Willie could take care of himself—but now Georgio Chinaglia is the first one there from the Cosmos, and he's kicking Willie while Willie's on the ground. I get there, grab Georgio, lift him off Willie and spin him away—right into Craven's fist. Cravo had just subbed in, hadn't even touched the ball, but he got there in time to plant one over Georgio's eye. And no, it wasn't an accident.

The referee breaks it up and ejects all four players. Eskandarian and Chinaglia go down the tunnel first. Then comes Willie, and as he rounds the turn toward the dressing rooms there's Georgio, screaming and throwing things against the wall. Georgio sees Willie and moves toward him (which for Willie is not good, because Georgio is a big man and he is clearly upset) but then Georgio hits the brakes so hard you can almost smell his cleats burning. Willie looks back over his shoulder—and there is Cravo. As he showed many times, if there was one guy in the NASL with whom Chinaglia wanted no fuss, it was Cravo. Georgio was a great player, a veritable scoring machine, but he never played well against us and two of the main reasons were Cravo and Kenyon. Even scoring, the physical price was too high. They knew the position, and they would put the boots to you.

Cravo was also a master needler because, when you played him, there was always the chance that when he'd finished playing with your head, he'd hand it to you.

Picture this: We're in the tunnel at Giants Stadium, side by side with the Cosmos, waiting for the player introductions, but there's some sort of delay and we're all just standing there. Suddenly, from the back of the line, Cravo cuts loose. And he is *screaming*:

"Who in the *bleep* do these bleeping bleepers think they *are?*" he storms, pointing at the Cosmos inches away. "Bleeping rich bleeping prima donnas! Big bleeping deal!"

Remember, now, these are the New York Cosmos of Beckenbauer, Chinaglia, Eskandarian and Johan Neeskens. They're superstars. They're used to opponents being awestricken, and here's this guy screaming at them like they're a bunch of ballboys! What would he do next? Frankly, I think he scared the shit out of them, but he was just having some fun jabbing the rich guys because . . . well, they *reacted* so well.

With Cravo, you never knew. Once, in the tunnel before a game against Washington, he started screaming at *me* because I was talking to Washington's Robert Iarusci. He was my teammate on the national squad, but tonight he's the opposition and I'm *talking* to him?? Cravo let me have it in no uncertain terms. I was pretty sure he was kidding—but I stopped talking.

Cravo thrived on contact and got away with a lot. Once I heard a smack, looked behind me as the ball went upfield, and this guy is lying there. He and Cravo had been going at it, and now he was in the dirt. Timing is everything, but there's always a price to be paid and Cravo never shied away from paying it.

Early in one game in Oakland against the Stompers he took a crack on the leg. We knew it had to be hurting badly, but he finished the game. It wasn't until he had X-rays at home the next day that we discovered he'd been playing on a broken leg.

There is a postscript to that story that also says a lot about the Elegant Thug. He was lost to us for the rest of the season and the playoffs, but he was there in his cast for Paul Nelson's first start in his place. When the coin flip put Nelson on the far side from the players' bench, Cravo grabbed a folding chair, hobbled around the track, set it up on the other sideline and proceeded to talk Nelson through the game. The crowd loved it, cheered him on, and booed the referee unmercifully when he informed Cravo that he and his chair would have to go. But to Cravo it made perfect sense. If he couldn't play, he'd coach. If he couldn't coach, he'd cheer. What's not to understand?

Cravo played three years for us and one more for the California Surf. He died suddenly in 1996 in Los Angeles at age forty-nine. Those angels had best keep their heads up.

John and Tony knew that, despite the successes of '77, we would have to be even better out of the gate in '78 lest we lose some of the more fickle among our increased fan base. We certainly gave the skeptics some early ammunition in our opener, getting smacked around at home 4–1 by San Diego, but there was always the sense on the team that we were going to be fine, because once they launched their talent hunt, John and Tony did not fool around.

Phil Parkes was back in goal after a year's absence. Defensively they landed Craven, Steve Harrison from Blackpool and Peter Daniel from Derby County. In midfield they grabbed Jon Sammels and Steve Kember, each of whom had more than 450 first division appearances to his credit.

Up front they went for royalty: "King" Kevin Hector, still a young thirty-three with more than 250 first division goals, mostly with Derby County, where he'd been a teammate of Hinton and Daniel. Okay, in marketing terms he wasn't the greatest interview. After our second home game, a 3–0 win over Seattle in which he'd set up one goal and scored another, reporters asked him how it felt.

"It's my job," he said as he packed away his boots.

Any other comment?

"No, thank you," he said politely, and headed for the door.

But he could put the ball in the net. At season's end he had 21 goals, so far ahead of anyone else on the squad he was in a different area code. I know this, because I was second with 10. What he also had was pride, never better proven than a decade later when his playing days were long behind him. A bunch of the English vets had been brought back for an anniversary game, the old Whitecaps vs. a team of ex-NASL players still living in the Pacific Northwest area. Given their advancing years and relative inactivity, they looked really good—so much so that the media guys were asking about it.

Kenyon had the answer.

"It's that bloody Kevin," he said. "He's had us working out and runnin' up and down flippin' hills for a couple of weeks. 'Those people treated us really well,' he said. 'We're not going over there and give them anything but our best.'"

The game had a classic moment. Craven, being Craven, was pounding everyone in sight. The second time that Ted McDougall, who'd played for Manchester United, took the brunt of it, he saw fit to protest.

"Jeez, Cravo," he said, "that was *late!*"

Mention the word "King" in Vancouver in 1978 or '79 and Vancouver soccer fans would add "Kevin Hector." Thirty-six goals in fifty-three games earned a lot of hugs. KENT KALLBERG

Cravo made a grudging concession to his age.
"It wasn't late when I started."

For me, it was a dream season, although one of change. We'd lost Bruce Wilson, who'd asked for a trade and, much to his surprise, wound up with the Chicago Sting, where he continued to play at his normal high level. Going in, we had no way of knowing that assistant coach Hinton would become a playmaking sensation. Buzzy was injured, so Tony had moved me from right back to midfield. Talk about being in the right place at the right time! Hinton kept dropping those balls off set pieces into the box, and it was like I had a ball magnet on my forehead. I had seventeen helpers myself to go with the 10 goals for a 37-point season, which won me the award as the league's North American player of the year, although not without a hitch and a boot to the bank account.

Ricky Davis of the New York Cosmos had won the award the previous year and collected $10,000 from the award sponsor. I was mentally figuring how I'd spend the money when the word came down: the award was now sponsored by an American magazine that had originally insisted that the competition be restricted to US players. There'd been a compromise: no restriction on who could win, but no prize money either. Bye-bye ten grand. I know, I know, it's the honour that counts, and I truly was honoured—but I'd have preferred to be honoured and up $10,000.

There was one moment, though, that far surpassed monetary value. It came in the second-last game of the regular season when we hammered San Jose 6–0. Sam and I had started and Danny had just subbed in—the three Lenarduzzi brothers playing together as we had through the countless growing-up hours, only this time it was in front of 24,000 fans at Empire Stadium. We can even tell our kids that we played a part in a goal. Mind you, so did everyone else. We passed the ball twenty-eight times in a row and every Whitecap touched the ball before it finally went in. It's nothing that will show in the record books, but for us it was a family assist.

Unfortunately, in the finale of a magical season in which we went 24–6, won our division, scored 68 goals (tied with Detroit and second only to the Cosmos, who led the NASL with 88) and averaged a shade over 15,000 fans at home, we reached into the top hat for the rabbit and pulled out a mouse.

It started well enough. We drew 30,811 to Empire Stadium to watch us stomp Toronto Blizzard 4–0 in the first round of the play-offs, and then we went to Portland and lost 1–0 to the Timbers in the first match of a best-of-three semi-final. Then, with 32,266 fans screaming their support in game two at home, we lost 2–0.

One goal in two games. It was going to be a long, long winter.

7

BIG DAY IN THE VILLAGE

"Vancouver must be like a deserted village right now."
—Jim McKay, ABC-TV, September 1, 1979

We knew going into the 1979 season that we had a good team. The playoff collapse of the previous season and the departure of Alan Hinton to coach in Tulsa left us a few potential miracles short, but John and Tony hadn't been sitting idle through the winter and some of the new blood looked promising.

It should have, because the Whitecaps paid to get it. The club executive, still with little or nothing in the way of profit to show for its investment, held a lengthy off-season board meeting and gave Tony the okay to go shopping. Naturally, he went first to England and came home with Kenyon, Willie Johnston, twenty-eight-year-old striker Trevor Whymark, Ray Lewington, a pit bull of a midfielder with flaming red hair and limitless desire who had just completed five years with Chelsea—and, oh, yes, an untested twenty-year-old named Carl Valentine from Oldham Athletic who left a vapour trail as he raced down the wing. "We thought he had some promise," Tony explained.

If anything, the drive to become accepted by the soccer enthusiasts intensified. If there was a charity or ethnic community event, Best made sure we had players there taking part. My brother Danny, Lofty Parkes and myself were male models in a fashion show fund-raiser (proceeds to the new children's hospital) that also included a Miss Bikini contest. Our players spoke to school groups, visited hospitals, manned phones for telethons. We weren't alone in this. The BC Lions and Vancouver Canucks were out there, too, although in the Canucks' case it wasn't that vital because in a hockey-mad province they had sellout crowds and a waiting list. For us it was part of a battle not just for acceptance but for survival, and John kept us on the front lines.

There was one promotion, however, that the team didn't like. In fact, it got our fine team photographer Kent Kallberg fired, although I'll never understand why.

It was a poster—of me. Kallberg got the idea and took the shot in the off-season after the '79 Soccer Bowl. T-shirt impresario Butts Giraud bought all the posters for sale in his stores, and the club fired Kent because he worked for the club and had done it on his own. For me, the project was a bit of a mystery. I realized that as a club original and local boy to boot I'd become a bit of a face for the franchise, which was fair enough, but a *poster*???

It did get publicity, most of it poking fun at the model.

"You haven't seen the Bobby Lenarduzzi poster?" Jim Taylor wrote in his *Province* sports column. "There are 5,000 of them around town, all aimed at helping young ladies through the difficult years when they're too old for Leif Garrett and too young for Burt Reynolds.

"It's done in Pin-Up Modern—full colour, jeans, open-throated shirt, gold chain, bracelet on the wrist, big smile showing the cute little broken tooth—everything but the staple in the navel . . .

"After careful study I've figured out why. Lenarduzzi's face hits both markets: the girls want to kiss it and the boys want to mess it up."

Oh, did I get ribbed about this. Hoping to ride the wave of our Soccer Bowl victory, team photographer Kent Kallberg produced this poster in the off-season. It did well, but some media suggested it might look better if I had a broken nose. KENT KALLBERG

It was not to be the last shot at my alleged good looks. Once, when I was struggling through a bad patch of playing, someone asked Tony what the problem was. "He needs a bottle in the face," he said, meaning that if my face was a tad more battered I'd be better able to concentrate on the game but that, as it was, I had too many distractions.

Tony meant nothing by it and probably regretted it as soon as it was out, but my mom went ballistic, to the point where Tony phoned her to apologize.

As for the posters, yes, I appeared at the stores to autograph them. They were out there and well publicized. Might as well use them to plug the club in the off-season. I took a lot of razzing, which was fair enough, but thankfully they've faded from memory over the years. Maybe the grown-up kids have trashed them. Maybe they're all gone. Well, almost all. Taylor kept one. Of course.

As for the playing season itself, we knew going in that things wouldn't be easy. Tony preached to us constantly that the NASL would be 30 percent stronger than in the previous year, which meant we had to be 30 percent stronger just to keep pace.

Still, Craven was back, and from the start he paired up with Kenyon as though they'd been born teammates and probably kicked the slats out of the same crib. Hector and Possee figured to be as dangerous as ever up front. I was on the move again, which was fine with me. I never cared much where I played as long as I was playing, which was probably a good thing. When Tony first arrived he moved me from centre half to right back. In 1978 I played four games there before being moved to left back and then back to midfield where I'd started. Now I was at left back again. Have cleats, will travel.

I looked at the side, and felt great. We had scoring power, we had solid goaltending and we had defence. There was reason for confidence, and we proved it by reaching the season's halfway point with a flourish, stomping the Cosmos 4–1 before 32,372 rabid fans at Empire Stadium—the first advance sellout in club history—to sit at a tidy 10–5.

They were still the Cosmos. We whipped them so badly—on goals by Hector, Sammels, Valentine and Possee—that they started arguing among themselves, and when Antonio Carbognani wouldn't stop berating the referee after getting a yellow card, Chinaglia ran over and kicked him in the butt.

Heady stuff, but there was a piece missing, and we didn't realize it until he arrived. His name was Alan Ball and, although our second-half season record merely matched our opening 10–5, we entered the playoffs on a roll. There was no doubt about the root cause of the difference. Ball was like a great symphony conductor: he led brilliantly and brought out the best in everyone.

For me, it was difficult not to stare at him open mouthed. This was a guy I'd watched on TV in my living room, England's youngest player in that controversial and historic World Cup Final win over Germany, the one that had cemented my desire to play professional soccer. Lord knows what the Philadelphia Fury, who had him on a loan contract, were thinking when they gave him up. Yes, he had sixteen years of wear and tear on a body that was listed as 5'8" and 140 pounds. Yes, he was thirty-four years old. But he was *Alan Ball*.

It was our assistant coach Bob McNab, who had been his teammate at Arsenal and knew he was unhappy in Philadelphia, that convinced Tony and John to go after him. They bought out his contract and, just like that, the legend was a Whitecap.

So here was my boyhood hero, this soccer icon, playing on my team, demanding the ball—and I wasn't giving it to him. It was one of his first games with us. I was playing right back and he'd come short looking for the ball and I wouldn't give it to him because with Tony the first option was always the up man and play from there. By halftime, he'd had enough and cornered me in the dressing room.

"When I'm coming to you for the ball, give it to me," he said. "I may give it right back to you but I'm looking to create space. If I'm asking, it's for a reason."

"But, what if there's a guy right up your ass," I protested.

"Don't worry about it," he said. "Just give me the ball."

Which, from then on, I did.

He wasn't a ball hog. He was the best passer I'd ever played with. Mostly his passes were short but you knew by the way the ball arrived exactly what he was telling you. If he put it ahead of you to run onto, you knew you had space. If it was at your feet it was in the right spot with the right weight for you to do what he could see was the best thing available to be done. He was absolutely amazing. He wasn't a physical player, he couldn't run fast or tackle much, but he had the intangible, unteachable something that set him apart. Alan Ball had vision.

He wasted no time proving it. In his first start, against the California Surf, his brilliant pass set up Willie's first goal of the season. Then, with no time left on the clock in extra time, he scored on his second try from the penalty spot after keeper Dave Jokerst had beaten him on his first attempt only to be called for moving early. One goal and one assist in a 2–1 victory, 3 points that matched his season output in eight games for the Fury.

Tony had been right: the regular season was brutally tough. Our depth saved us because our regulars were falling with alarming regularity. We didn't get the division title clinched until the second-last game of the season, when Whymark scored in sudden-death overtime for a 1–0 win over the San Jose Earthquakes.

It was a season laced with bruises and memories, the greatest being that return match against the Cosmos I mentioned earlier, the one where Craven, Johnston, Eskandarian and Chinaglia were all ejected after their celebrated brawl and each received the automatic suspension for their team's next game. That one deserves a second look, because it shows how Cosmo-centric the NASL had become and how arrogant were the people at Warner Brothers, who owned the franchise—yes, the same wonderful folk who brought us Porky Pig, Wile E. Coyote and the Roadrunner. Believe it or not, the Cosmos announced they damned well were going to play Eskandarian and Chinaglia in their next game, against the Minnesota Kicks, no matter what the rules said.

The newspaper quotes were interesting:

"We're going to use the two players who were thrown out. I

don't like what people are doing to the Cosmos, including the commissioner of the NASL!"—Julio Mazzei, Cosmos technical director.

"Get the blankety-blank away from me . . . and get that blankety-blank commissioner in my office at nine tomorrow!"—Jay Emmett, Warner's executive, to NASL director of operations Ted Howard.

The ultimatum drew headlines all over North America. Phil Woosnam vs. Bugs Bunny, screamed the *Vancouver Province*, and sarcastically raised and answered a key question: "Would the creators of Tweety Bird do something wrong? Of course not."

What should have happened, of course, is that Woosnam should have hit Mazzel and Emmett with hefty fines. Do you think he wouldn't have done it to Capozzi and Best if they'd been the ones doing the screaming? You think he wouldn't have levelled an additional suspension if it had been Craven or Willie who ripped the red card out of referee Keith Styles' hand and hurled it to the ground, as did Chinaglia?

What happened? Nothing. The Cosmos didn't use Chinaglia and Eskandarian against Minnesota and that ended it, for the moment. But if we and the Cosmos should meet in the playoffs . . .

We had a little extra incentive heading into the first round against the Dallas Tornado, whose coach, Al Miller, was quoted as calling us "thugs," aiming in large measure at Cravo without preceding it with the Elegant. Okay . . .

Into Dallas's tiny Ownby Stadium we went, and built a 2–0 lead on goals by Valentine and Parsons only to have them come back to tie it. Then Tony made a key move, indicating to the hurt and hobbling Lewington that he was about to be replaced—and he *hated* being subbed. Before Tony could make the move, Lewington took a pass from Hector and scored what proved to be the winning goal.

At Empire, the Tornado didn't get a shot on goal until early in the second half, but it went into the net. Then came what you might call poetic justice. Cravo, who'd been slowed all year by injuries, tied the score on a relay from Hector and, just over a minute later, got his head on Ball's perfect cross and knocked home the eventual winner. In the final twenty-five minutes Dallas got one shot. How do you like the thug now, Mr. Miller?

That put us against the Los Angeles Aztecs in the most emotional playoff I've ever been involved in. It didn't hit me until the second game.

These were the Aztecs of the fabulous Johan Cruyff and the Royal Dutch Air Force, a tag given in tribute to the height of its Dutch players. Not only had we failed to beat them in one pre-season game, we'd been shut out twice in the regular season. Now we'd opened the playoffs in Los Angeles, blown a 2–0 early lead on a pair by Valentine by giving up two late goals, struggled scoreless through overtime and lost the match in the shootout, highlighted

Getting through the NASL playoffs was a long, hard task. For Lofty Parkes, the western division title called for a swig of champagne and a peck on the cheek for Derek Possee. KENT KALLBERG / BC SPORTS HALL OF FAME AND MUSEUM

Not sure whether I jumped this high or whether I was launched by Bob Sibbald (2) before I could get in shooting position for a go at Colin Boulton. The playoff win was worth the landing jolt. BC SPORTS HALL OF FAME AND MUSEUM

by an unbelievable goal by Cruyff. If ever our fans had a right to be disenchanted, it was when we came home for game two.

As we ran out of the tunnel onto the pitch, I got goosebumps. Empire was jammed, and 32,375 fans weren't yelling at us, they were yelling *to* us, screaming that we could take these guys and win the mini-game and the series. They cheered, they chanted, they sang. It was raw emotion, and we drank it in like wine. How could we *not* win for these people?

We were unbelievably disciplined and, after a scoreless first half, we got lucky. Galindo Sanchez steered a ticketed shot by Hector off the line only to have the ball hit one of his own players and carom into the net. The goal stood up, and we took the ten-minute break before the mini-game that would decide the series.

In the stands it was bedlam without a second's break, but that was nothing compared to the noise level three minutes after the opening whistle of the mini-game when Whymark's pass found Valentine deep on the right flank, Carl made the cross and Hector, high in the air and parallel to the turf, headed it in for the lead. I was right behind him and if he hadn't headed it in I would have. Again we shut them down the rest of the way, and there we were, National Conference champions for the first time ever.

We were one hurdle away from the Soccer Bowl game. Standing in the way: Chinaglia, Beckenbauer, Eskandarian, Alberto and probably Bugs, Porky, Tweety and Yosemite Sam.

We didn't care. We'd beaten the Cosmos in both regular-season meetings. We viewed them with respect, not fear. We'd get them at Empire in the first game of the series, and after all the years of struggle when no one cared or came to watch—the years when Best would hit every ethnic association dinner or dance wherever soccer people gathered and open with "I'm John Best from the Whitecaps," then make a motion as though taking off his hat and say, "Now I'm

Coaches Julio Mazzei and Tony Waiters were all smiles as we opened the '79 playoff series with the New York Cosmos at Empire Stadium, but the showdown became an all-out war. KENT KALLBERG

John Best from Liverpool. Tell me why you won't come to see us play?"—the city was ours!

Tickets for the Wednesday night opener went on sale at 9 a.m. Monday. The line started to form shortly after midnight. By mid-morning it was four city blocks long. Other outlets were just as busy. Scalpers—an NASL game and we had *scalpers*?—did their usual damage and by Monday evening every ticket was gone with hundreds still waiting in line.

John Best gulped and made a gutsy decision. He lifted the TV blackout to allow the telecast to be carried live in the local market. There was a risk. Fans who'd stood in line through the night and day for tickets might resent the fact that people who didn't could sit at home and watch the game in comfort for free and get replays. They might opt to stay home themselves and, come next year, they might remember at renewal time.

But John had faith. True soccer fans want to see the game live, he insisted. They want to *be there*. And he was right. The no-shows were minimal. The announced crowd was 32,875—and we gave them a show.

The first half ended scoreless, although we out-shot them 12–2. In the second half, naturally, all hell broke loose.

The Cosmos tried to apply pressure but Craven and Kenyon were both healthy now and nothing was getting past them. You could sense the frustration. All that talent and they couldn't score on this team whose total wages probably didn't match Beckenbauer's? What the hell?

Willie put us ahead by slipping inside, where he was seldom found, to throw himself at Ball's cross and pound the ball home. With fifteen minutes left, after Lofty had twice foiled Dennis Tueart on good shots, Ball worked his magic again with a quick pass that turned Whymark loose on a breakaway. Trevor put the ball between Hubert Birkenmeier's legs for the 2–0 lead and we were home and dry.

The Cosmos did not take it well. Two were cautioned for rough play and with just eight seconds left on the clock Eskandarian was ejected for chopping down Hector. And still it wasn't over. As the Cosmos headed for the locker room, Carlos Alberto threw his shirt at a linesman, then spat in his face. The red card was automatic, which meant Alberto would have to miss the second game in New York three days later. Arrogant to the end, the Warner Brothers people protested the one-game penalty, and threatened to use him anyway and sue the league if it wasn't allowed. They never followed through, and I'm guessing they were stunned that the threat alone wasn't enough to have the league knuckle under.

That game, by the way, was memorable for me in a miserable sort of way for another reason. I was against a Portuguese international named Polimene Seninho, a right winger with jets like I'd never faced before. The guy should have been an Olympic sprinter. He was giving me a rough time, but near the end they took him off for some reason.

"Good thing, too," Tony said to me later. "If they hadn't, I was going to take YOU off."

"Well," I admitted, "if you had, I'd have had no grounds for complaint."

So we go to NY for what turns out to be the longest game in NASL history. I spend most of the flight wondering how I'm going to handle Seninho, who'd already proved he was so much faster than me that it must have looked like I was standing in quicksand. Sure enough, ten minutes into the match the ball was played in behind me, he cut it over, Chinaglia put them up 1–0 and I thought it might be the beginning of the end.

Lofty held us in and we got one back—again it was Ball with a brilliant free kick that found Craven—but with seven minutes left in the half Chinaglia scored again.

In retrospect, the respective strategies were interesting. The Cosmos weren't worried about trailing the series. They'd lost their semifinal opener 3–0 to the Roughnecks in Tulsa, then come home to crush them 3–0 to knot the series and 3–1 in the mini-game to win it. Scoring was their game. They'd swarm us early, get a comfortable lead, then relax and conserve their energy for the mini-game.

Tony anticipated the plan and didn't mind at all. His own plan was to force the Cosmos to keep up their early frantic pace, to press them so they couldn't take it easy and let what he considered to be our superior conditioning wear them down. In his mind, being down by one at the half was no big deal—as long as his theory about superior conditioning winning the day proved correct.

It took a while, but it did, sort of. For the second straight game Willie snuck inside, which was pretty much foreign territory for him. I got a cross in to him and he headed it in to tie it at 2–2 just minutes from the end of regulation time. Unfortunately, we couldn't find the net in overtime, and now the game would be decided by a shootout.

As I've mentioned before, we didn't do well at shootouts. We'd won only one all year. You could almost hear the Cosmos snickering as they won this one in four rounds to send the playoffs into a deciding mini-game.

We didn't panic. Yes, as Willie said the first time he ran into the NASL rule, "Losing is bad, but losing in a shootout is soul destroying" and now we'd just lost another. However, as Tony kept telling us, the day was still ours to win, and the conditioning factor was beginning to take its toll on the Cosmos, who had Johan Neeskens and Tueart hobbling.

The first fifteen minutes of the mini-game ended scoreless. Then Valentine ripped down the left side and fired a shot over Birkenmeier's shoulder. The ball smashed into the underside of the crossbar, came straight down, and bounced out. Beckenbauer headed it over the back line, but the linesman was signalling Goal!

The referee looked at him for confirmation and the guy nodded that, yes, it was a goal. We were ahead and a few minutes from the league final! Jubilantly we lined up for the kickoff.

But wait—Chinaglia was nose to nose with the linesman, screaming that the ball had not been completely over the goal line and maybe reminding him that they were the Cosmos and who paid his salary? Whatever. The guy changed his mind and signalled a goal kick, which was wrong on two counts, firstly because the goal had already been awarded, and secondly because if it *wasn't* a goal it was a corner kick because Kaiser Franz had headed it over the end line.

But, goal kick it was. And what was settled? Nothing, The mini-game ended scoreless, and once again the whole thing would be decided by a shootout. And then it got really insane.

Tony juggled his shootout lineup. In the first one, I'd been the only one to beat Birkenmeier as we lost 3–1, so this time I went first, followed by Bolitho, Valentine, Ball and Possee. I got lucky again and we were never worse than tied through the next three shooters. Now it was tied 2–2 and up stepped Possee.

We couldn't have asked for a better choice. In the clutch, Derek was unflappable. He was also more than a little bit ticked off at being left out of the first shootout, because we'd been practising them all week and he hadn't missed one, but Derek was a pro in every sense of the word. Watching the shootout as it progressed, he noticed that on every shot Birkenmeier charged out to around the penalty spot, cutting down the shooter's angle as he raced in from the 35-yard line as NASL rules required. As he prepared to go out for the biggest shot of his life, he turned to Buzzy. "I'm going to chip him," he said.

"You sure?" Buzzy gulped. Trying to chip the ball over a charging goalie rather than blast one past him was great if you made it. If you didn't, you looked like an idiot. And what if Birkenmeier *didn't* come out? What then?

"He's charging out *every time*," Possee insisted. "I'm chipping it."

Possee pushed the ball ahead and moved in. Right on cue, Birkenmeier charged out to cut off the angle, and Derek calmly chipped the ball high over his head and into the net to give us the lead. Now it was down to Neisi Morais against Parkes. If he scores, the shootout continues. If Lofty beats him, we win.

But wait a minute. Remember the catch in the shootout rules? Attacking players will start with the ball on the 35-yard line and must take their shot within five seconds.

Morais must have forgotten. He took the ball toward Parkes, then veered right to get a better angle and fired the ball into what was now an open net. But the big five-second clocks were ticking down and, as even the Cosmo fans could see, they hit 0 an instant

Dynamite can come in small packages. Derek Possee turned giant in the shootout with a gutsy shootout chip over Cosmos goalie Hubert Birkenmeier that put us in the Soccer Bowl. KENT KALLBERG

before he took the shot! Now the boot is on the other foot, because the Cosmos are jumping up and down, thinking they've scored to tie it at three each, but there was the referee, pointing to the clock and waving it off!

We'd finally won a shootout and a trip to the Soccer Bowl with it! We were hugging and backslapping—but Tony just sat there at the bench, making sure this one wasn't going to be changed the way Valentine's had. When it was official, when the game was over and beyond Cosmo arguments, filibusters or lobbying, or attack by the entire Warner Brothers menagerie, *then* he allowed himself a grin and joined the celebration.

The game had gone to the maximum time and it was on ABC TV, and the result moved Jim McKay to make his famous "village of Vancouver" remark. It was no big deal. The man was a world-famous announcer and a consummate professional. Okay, "village" was an unfortunate word choice, but all he was saying was that everyone in Vancouver must be agog at what American-based media, including his network, would consider a huge upset. Nonetheless, back home in the village the overreaction was instantaneous. *Village, eh? Stick that up your big-city New York arse!*

We didn't know, of course, and wouldn't have cared. In a week, we'd be playing in the Soccer Bowl against Tampa Bay, right there in New York! We flew home on the Sunday, Tony gave us the next day off, we practised at Empire Tuesday and flew back to New York on Wednesday—all but Lofty, Hector and Ball, who left a day early to meet league commitments and attend Commissioner Woosnam's press conference.

We were not welcome back at Giants Stadium. Clearly we'd spoiled the plans of thousands of fans who'd purchased Soccer Bowl tickets on the assumption that their beloved Cosmos would be in it, not some bunch of interlopers from north of the 49th parallel. Judging from the total ticket sale (66,843) and actual attendance (50,699), some 16,000 of them were so pissed off they didn't even bother

Ooh, this must have hurt. Cosmos' scoring ace Georgio Chinaglia gives Tony a congratulatory handshake after we'd spoiled their (and Warner Bros.) title plans. Sorry, Bugs. KENT KALLBERG

to come out—probably stayed home and watched Warner Brothers cartoons. Tough carrots, Bugs.

Most of those who did come made it their business to make sure we knew we weren't welcome. They booed us during warm-up, they booed even more loudly during our player introductions, and a bunch behind our bench booed us through the entire match. One woman screamed obscenities at us, start to finish, through the first half. No word was too vile. Finally, when she could stand it no more, she leaped to her feet, screaming and shaking her fist, and it was as if the Good Lord had heard enough. Her skirt fell off. I don't know how or why—maybe it caught on a nail as she rose—but it just ripped off and there she was, skirtless.

It says something about our club that we were totally focused. We'd had a rough week. Our core English players had complained to

New York fans, who'd expected to see their beloved Cosmos in the Soccer Bowl, weren't too happy to see us parading it up and down the field after beating the Rowdies 2–1 for the title. KENT KALLBERG

John and Tony over the lack of a bonus from the club for reaching the final, which was common practice back home. In their view the Soccer Bowl prize money was ludicrous—$2,500 per man for the winners and $1,500 apiece for the losers. Guys like Ball, who'd been in big finals before, snorted that they could make that much at home flogging their free match tickets. They wanted a bonus, and that was that.

Two things we didn't realize at the time: that the no-bonus rule was an NASL edict over which the team had no control; and that, for many of our English veterans, the ill feelings the decision generated would linger in the Whitecaps structure like a cancer.

We'd barely gotten into our celebration for chopping down the Cosmos before John Best got the call from league headquarters. The NASL view was that bonuses would be handled by the league, that the prize money for getting into the Soccer Bowl was sufficient, and that neither the Whitecaps nor the Rowdies were to shell out any further rewards on pain of league sanction. A call to Gordon Jago of Tampa Bay confirmed that he'd received a similar call and a similar warning. No bonuses, period.

Hands tied, Best approached his board of directors looking for some way around the problem. They essentially told the complainers to go pound sand. They didn't need to go looking for an angle. The players had contracts. They could bloody well live up to them. There were a couple of bitch sessions to discuss the next move but the owners stood firm. No bonuses. We did, however, get *lovely* medallions embossed with the Soccer Bowl crest. Apparently it was supposed to go on a chain, which wasn't included. I gave mine to my mom, who passed it on to Deanne when we married.

For the Canadian players the fuss was foreign territory. Money had never been an issue. How could it? We'd never made enough to live off the game. I remember coming home after that first $100-a-week season in Reading and talking bravely to my family about having to get more as a second-year man, but in the end I got a trifle *less*. When the Whitecaps went full-time in 1978 I was making $1,000 a *month*. I loved living at home but the truth of it is, at those wages I couldn't have afforded to live anywhere else. So when all the tough talk surfaced before Soccer Bowl we just kind of shrugged, listened and went along.

It could have been disruptive, but it wasn't. Not that day, anyway. This wasn't a team of Goody Twoshoes. We didn't have angels, and there was a lot of drinking and carousing on road trips. It could be argued that, in terms of deportment, some of them weren't the best of role models but when it was time to work, it was time to work. There was a job to do and, until it was done, nothing else mattered.

Ball pulled a few of the young guys aside in the dressing room and gave us the word: "You're going to remember this day for the rest of your lives," he said, "so let's make it a good day. You may think you're going to get to a lot more finals, and I hope you do,

He feigned pregnancy with a soccer ball under his jersey and waddled out when his name was called, but once the whistle blew, Willie Johnston showed the Tampa Bay Rowdies' Manny Andruszewski how serious he could be. KENT KALLBERG

but you might not. So savour the moment and enjoy it." I will never forget the way he took the field.

We were all fighting the butterflies in our own way. When Lofty was introduced, he raced out onto the field blowing mock kisses to the New York fans he knew were there to see him fail. Willie stuffed a soccer ball under his jersey and waddled out like an expectant mother eight months along.

The rest of us charged out. Alan Ball walked.

I can still see the walk—head up, shoulders back, striding across the artificial turf, no sign of a strut, just an office worker heading for his desk. As the *Vancouver Province* put it the following day: *He reminded you instead of the old bull listening to the young one demanding that they run down the hill and do one of the heifers. And the old bull said he had a better idea. "Let's walk down," he said, "and do 'em all."*

"You're going to remember this day for the rest of your lives," Alan Ball told us before the big game, "so let's make it a good day." Then, all business, he walked out onto the field to get at it. KENT KALLBERG

As for the game itself, well, "anti-climactic" isn't quite the right word, but there was a strange feel to it because we'd come away from the same field a week earlier having played a four-and-a-half-hour marathon to get past the Cosmos. Now it wasn't so much a case of overconfidence as of having pretty much seen everything and knowing how we had to play this time to get it done.

Whymark got us the early lead and the winner after the Rowdies had equalized, both set up on heady, no-frills passes from Ball. And in the eighty-ninth minute, as he was about to take a throw-in at their end of the pitch, he made a motion to Willie with instructions crystal clear: keep possession, go to the corner and kill the clock, which Willie did for about forty-five seconds. He had the ball in his hands for a throw-in when the whistle blew.

Truth is, it wasn't much of a game. We didn't give them many opportunities or take a lot of chances ourselves. "We won today because we didn't attempt anything we weren't capable of doing," Ball

No one had more right to celebrate than Trevor Whymark (9) as he and Ray Lewington waved the trophy at New Yorkers. He scored both our goals and was named the game's outstanding offensive player. KENT KALLBERG

It is one of the game's great traditions: Exchange jerseys with the team you've lost to or beaten. Seconds after our Soccer Bowl win, John Craven was wearing Manny Andruszewski's. KENT KALLBERG

What a finish for his rookie season. Steve Nesin (R) gets to grasp the Soccer Bowl with two old guys who'd been waiting forever: me and Buzz Parsons. KENT KALLBERG

Not to turn his back on GM John Best (back), but when Dr. Henry Kissinger came to the dressing room to offer congratulations, Buzz was quick to grab a shot for his memory book. KENT KALLBERG

Herb Capozzi (left) always thought big when he formed the Whitecaps in '74. Now he and director Peter Webster got to hold proof that dreams do come true. KENT KALLBERG

told the assembled media later. "We just did the things we do best, and did them well."

Hey, entertainment is a secondary factor in the final of any sport, and the crowd wasn't with us anyway. And who left the pitch with the Soccer Bowl? In the changing room later, who was a gracious Dr. Henry Kissinger congratulating?

We were Soccer Bowl champions, but New York had one more curve ball to throw at us.

We get back to our hotel to celebrate—and find all our bags stacked in the lobby, which is full of old guys, mostly white haired and some with crew cuts. It was the old story. The hotel hadn't planned on us being there anyway. It was the Cosmos who, as everyone in New York knew for certain, would be in the championship game, and they'd be in no need of accommodations. When we spoiled that plan, the hotel had managed to find rooms for us, but for only one night. Our rooms were now occupied by attendees at a convention of the Veterans of Foreign Wars.

Had we lost the match and the Soccer Bowl, there might have been trouble (as it was, Lofty had a desk clerk pinned to the wall), but in the end we just moved on to the Holiday Inn, partied the night away and flew home the next day.

And after all that, there was dessert. On the flight home our PR man, Jack Leonard, informed us there'd be a welcome-home parade and passed out maps of the route.

We just looked at one another. The Soccer Bowl wasn't exactly the Stanley Cup or the Grey Cup. What if they gave a parade and nobody came?

We needn't have worried. We were swarmed at the airport. On the parade route the cheers were deafening. Crowd estimates varied but most figured about 100,000 lined the streets and you couldn't have crammed another fan into Robson Square, where it concluded, without a shoehorn. All I know is that there were people hanging from lampposts trying to get a better view of the players as the open convertibles wove slowly through the streets, and that if everyone who's claimed over the years that they attended the parade actually *did*, the total would have been doubled.

I'm not sure there's ever been a crowd like that, not even when the Lions won the Grey Cup. Maybe the year the Canucks *didn't* win the Stanley Cup. Probably the crowds in the streets during the

Winter Olympics were thicker, but they were for a festival, not a welcome-home party.

Fairy tale stuff, and to me it exemplified our season. No one could have predicted it. Who would have dared to suggest that it would end with a parade covered live by the CBC or that Vancouver mayor Jack Volrich would shout into a microphone as the party ran down that "We're going to build a stadium!"

We were champions, and things could only get better. Why would we not think so? We'd had 10,000 season ticket holders this season. And in the first ten days after the win over the Cosmos, before we'd even played the Soccer Bowl game, the club processed requests for 7,500 more for next season. *New* customers, not old. What could go wrong?

We were about to find out.

When we heard there'd be a parade to celebrate the Soccer Bowl title, we wondered if anyone would bother to come out. About 100,000 did, looking for autographs and maybe (gasp!) a chance to touch the trophy. KENT KALLBERG / BC SPORTS HALL OF FAME AND MUSEUM

8

THE VIEW FROM THE OUTHOUSE AIN'T PRETTY

*"Coming out of the stadium after the Soccer Bowl
victory I noticed a lot of people hanging around the
players' entrance. They were agents looking for clients.
That's really where the trouble started."*
                                        —John Best, 2011

It was 1984, and Deanne was driving me to the Whitecaps' office
to face Lord-only-knew-what.

The NASL was in its death throes but, as I kept telling myself, that was nothing new. Okay, we'd lost three teams for the 1981
season, *seven* teams for 1982, two more for 1983 and three more
for 1984, which meant we were down to . . . don't think about it,
Bobby! Be positive!

Well, let's see. Hadn't the league dropped from seventeen teams
to five in 1969? And didn't it survive? This wasn't *that* bad.

Still, franchises had been bouncing around like Ricochet Rabbit, two of them landing in Western Canada, courtesy of two well-
known promoters. Nelson Skalbania bought the Memphis Rogues
and made them the Calgary Boomers. The Oakland Stompers, who
became the Connecticut Bicentennials, who became the Hartford

Bicentennials, were morphed into the Edmonton Drillers by Edmonton Oilers' owner Peter Pocklington. Now the two men shared *two* claims to fame: each had had an NASL franchise collapse, and each had signed Wayne Gretzky and sold him.

It wasn't just the in-and-gone teams we'd lost, clubs whose names you'd barely had time to remember. Warner Brothers had pulled out of the Cosmos (bye-bye, Bugs), who were now led by a group fronted by Chinaglia and, for the first time since 1976, did not lead the league in attendance in 1983. Seattle Sounders—the *Sounders!*—whom John Best had built into a bedrock franchise, had folded after the 1983 season. What did *that* tell you?

Team owners also seemed more interested in concentrating on the fall-winter indoor game, which was cheaper to run. It was as if they were intent on proving they'd learned absolutely nothing from the outdoor expansion fiasco and could still screw up a one-car funeral. They'd succeeded beyond belief.

The indoor league opened in 1979–80 with ten teams playing a twelve-game schedule. The following season—does this sound familiar?—it expanded to *nineteen* teams and bumped the team season to eighteen games. By opening day of '81–'82, six teams had folded, then the '82–'83 season was cancelled and after a seven-team comeback attempt in '83–'84 the whole thing was scrapped.

(For the record, even the Whitecaps got involved for two years, with minor success. Basically, though, the local soccer community's interest in the indoor game was nicely summed up by a fan who said, "Trust the NASL. They've figured a way to get people to pay to watch an indoor practice!")

Still, there had to be a way! We'd played with nine teams last season. We could do it again. Sure, we could! That's assuming all nine teams came back, and I wasn't even sure that *this one* was. What if . . . damn it, mind, *shut up!*

Even as the car pulled up to the Whitecaps' office I was telling myself things were going to be all right. They had to be! This team had been my life! If the league folded and the team went with it, as it surely would, how would I support myself, my wife and our year-old baby son, Ryan? Soccer was the only profession I'd ever had. I'd just turned thirty, and even if I tried to go back to England, how many teams would be wanting a thirty-year-old from Canada whose body already had all that soccer mileage?

JOB WANTED. Thirty-year-old who can kick with either foot seeks new employment opportunity. No previous experience in any field without goalposts . . .

Oh, yeah, that would work.

I squared my shoulders, mentally crossed my fingers, and went in to face The Man.

Almost all the old faces had changed. Capozzi was still chairman of the board, but very much in the background. Best had moved back to the Sounders as GM early in the 1982 season and got them into the NASL final, only to lose to the Cosmos. With his usual great timing, he left before the 1983 season when new owners took over and thus missed the collapse. Tony was coaching the national team full-time. I was working for a band of strangers led by one J. Bob Carter, who'd been a member of the club's executive and one day found himself the only one left. He'd just finished his first year, lost a bundle, and apparently had decided to stop the bleeding. Jim Fleming, the man he'd put in charge of the operation, reluctantly gave me the word.

"We're looking at the bottom line," he said, "and we can't commit to a contract for next year."

It was like someone kicked me in the testicles. I felt *empty*. In a few hours I'd be worrying about things like a job and bills and putting food on the table but now, as Deanne drove us home, I just felt numb.

For the rest of the team, all as anxious as I was, it was a signal. I was the original guy, the long-time face of the franchise. If I couldn't get a contract, the team was done. Sure enough, in a matter of days, the franchise was folded—which became academic a short time later when the entire league went toes-up with us. But that didn't make it hurt any less.

So what went wrong? How could a championship team that pulled 100,000 cheering fans into the streets for a victory parade after the 1979 season be out of business four years later?

Part of it, I think, was amnesia. We forgot how tough it had been to build our fan base and how hard we'd worked to win acceptance by the soccer community. Who needed to send players out to speak and sign autographs and keep our faces and our team in the public eye, as we had since the day John Best arrived? In 1980, still riding the title wave of the year before, we averaged 28,000 per game and had 22,000 season tickets. All we had to do was show up and play! Wrong. *Really* wrong.

Hindsight, of course, is easy, but I think we also misread the nature of that magical connection between our fans and that championship team. Teams that don't make moves go stagnant. Our fans knew that. What management didn't realize—and who could blame them, because it defied the just-win-baby fan attitude that was the very bedrock of any sport you could name—was the uniqueness of our supporters' relationship with the veterans who'd led us to the title. Given a choice between improving the side and going one more season with the aging veterans they'd come to love, they'd likely have preferred a struggling team with them to an improved team without.

However, that wasn't what did in the franchise. The truth of it, I suspect, is that it started to die the week before the Soccer Bowl game, when our English vets found out there would be no bonuses for getting to the championship. The resentment festered, the poison got into the bloodstream and the patient succumbed to terminal pique.

Best had seen it coming and tried to head it off. He'd offered to hold training camp for the 1980 season in Hawaii and to bring the players' families at club expense. He'd extended or bumped up every player's contract, no matter what year it was in. Nothing worked. The malcontents remained unhappy and obviously planned to stay that way.

There were two other issues: player agents, and Alan Ball.

The agents were circling almost before the Soccer Bowl referee could get the final whistle to his lips. A lot of players had agents, and that was fine. I had a great one in Ron Perrick. The problem was the new sharks who were circling, smelling a sport on the upsurge and, of course, their own percentage of whatever they could get for whatever players they could sign. Mostly they had represented people in the entertainment industry. Some had never represented an athlete in any sport, let alone in soccer. One of them landed Lofty Parkes.

Best and Tony wanted to re-sign Lofty and, as Best said later, it would have been a perfect move for both sides. Everybody loved Lofty. At thirty-three his playing time was running out, but staying with the Whitecaps, particularly with Waiters running the show (an ex-keeper and a first-class one at that), Lofty's chances for longevity would be much greater than if he moved on.

The agent's demands, Best said, were ludicrous—hundreds of thousands of dollars—made by a man who clearly had no understanding of the soccer marketplace. When he wouldn't budge, Best reluctantly put Lofty on the market. Chicago made the best offer, and there went our keeper and one of the lynchpins of our championship club. He stayed a year and a bit with the Sting, moved on to San Diego for a half-season, then drifted to the Oklahoma City Slickers of the American Soccer League before coming back to the NASL for one game with Toronto in 1983. And that was it. Would he have been better off staying with the Whitecaps? Who knows? But we lost a fine player and team man, the first of what turned out to be an exodus, partly through resentment and partly because Best could see no way it could ever be solved. "So," he now recalls, "I pulled the trigger."

His reasoning was simple: a disgruntled team would be more likely to fall apart than to win. In the NASL, it would take three years to build a contender. So, if changes had to be made, do it sooner rather than later.

After much media speculation, Kevin Hector was gone, partly as the result of a contract dispute and partly because management felt that his age had begun to show during an injury-plagued season. Jon Sammels, our captain throughout much of '79 and understandably upset about being shelved for the big game, left for England at the first opportunity and never returned. Willie Johnston, his one-year FIFA exile over, had resumed his career in Glasgow.

Alan Ball was back but clearly didn't want to be, and wouldn't have been but for his existing contract. He'd agreed to return to Blackpool and take over as player/manager once his summer league commitments to the Whitecaps were over. Blackpool's management, eager to have him in place early, even offered to come over, train in Canada and play an exhibition against the Whitecaps. Ball, they said, could train with us, then leave and go to train with Blackpool. When Best declined this generous offer to provide Blackpool with a Canadian summer holiday, Ball ran the Blackpool side by remote control through his assistant, Ted MacDougall. His attitude and on-field effort left no doubt where his heart was, and I remembered Bob McNab's words when he was urging the club to get him from Philadelphia.

"Bally will be good for the short term," he told me. "Not for the long haul."

He called it. Bally appeared in sixteen games and contributed two goals and three assists. He'd been our catalyst, but now he didn't seem to care and was gone the instant he could be.

We came to camp in '80, and everything had changed.

Tony wasn't the head coach anymore, although he was still involved. McNab had moved up from assistant to the top job and inherited a hornet's nest. In '79 we'd been tight as a drum. Now we had factions. It didn't take long for us to realize it just wasn't going to work.

Poor Bob. He was a fine coach, but he was also a fitness fanatic whose answer to the discontent was to run a camp that ran his players to a total frazzle. A lot of them didn't like it. By the end of pre-season, guys were dying out there. Seven or eight games in he was gone and Tony was back, but a season that started badly only got worse.

I had problems of my own, mostly self-created. In the off-season

I'd hit the post-title banquet circuit pretty hard. Everyone wanted some view of the Whitecaps and I'd been happy to oblige but now, as I trotted out for our first league game, I heard a smattering of boos as my name was announced.

"What's that about," asked Ray Hankin, one of our new signings.

"Don't know," I replied. Boos weren't something I was used to hearing at home games. I think part of it was fans' reaction to my over-exposure in the off-season. They'd had enough of me. Since I wasn't playing well, I couldn't especially blame them. I was a real target and I was struggling, so they were quick to have a go.

Then I got benched for a friendly game against Nott's Forest. I'd never *been* benched, and it didn't sit well. As I flopped down on the substitutes' bench, a leather-lunged fan gave it to me.

"Hey, Lenarduzzi!" he yelled. "Welcome to the cheap seats!"

I remember thinking: "I'm gonna *kill* that sunuvabitch!" but I resisted the temptation to turn around, which would just have given him a reason to stay on me. All in all, a humbling experience.

Management was trying, I'll give them that. They paid a good chunk to get Hankin, and probably more to get the Dutch legend Rudy Krol, who arrived with great talent and even greater confidence. After fourteen games he was sold back to Napoli.

It was that kind of a year. Nothing went right. The crowds held up, but we finished at 16–16 and got swept in both games by the Sounders in the first round of the playoffs.

Our next coach, and as it turned out our last, was John Giles, who arrived in '81, a legend in his own right with a style all his own. During his long playing career he was named the Republic of Ireland's all-time greatest player. He was such a force with Leeds United from 1963 through 1975 that Alf Ramsay, in assessing his England side's potential heading into what was to be a championship World Cup run in 1966, lamented:

"As I look at the talent at my disposal today, my one regret is that John Giles wasn't born an Englishman."

Giles' training sessions were five-a-side with a high intensity level, but he was not a details guy who'd spend a lot of time in front of a blackboard or practising free kicks. Nonetheless, I later took something from his approach when I began my own coaching career.

He'd watch the workouts as they were handled by an assistant, then pull a player out to speak to him individually. He spoke softly and simply, and the message was always short: you need to do this better or do that better, or let's tidy up this part of your game. It was great communication and, as a player, I loved it. Then came a series of games in which I was never called out. I'd thought I was playing pretty well, but with no word from the coach I was starting to doubt it. Then, one afternoon, he did. It took all of ten seconds.

"I haven't called you out because I didn't need to," he said. "You're doing everything I want."

And that was that. I was on cloud nine, which made me appreciate something: when you're the head coach, *communicate*, and not just to the ones who aren't performing. Remember to let players know when they're doing well, even if it's just a quick "Well done!" Yes, concentrate on the team as a whole, but don't forget the individuals.

On the field, Giles snapped us back to a 21–11 record in 1981, only to be humiliated yet again in the first round of the playoffs by Tampa Bay, 4–1 on the road and 1–0 at home in front of 28,896 fans.

In 1982, more of the same: third in our division at 20–12 and another first-round playoff exit in three games with San Diego, losing 5–1 on the road, winning 1–0 at home and losing 2–1 in the decider in San Diego. In 1983 we suffered a final blow in a season that might otherwise have given us a chance.

We thought we had a shot at the Soccer Bowl, which could be critical because it was being played on our new home ground, the 60,000-seat BC Place domed stadium, where we'd played Seattle on July 23 in the first event ever held there and won 2–1 before a sold-out house of 60,342. Never mind that the league was on life support—get to the Soccer Bowl and we might turn things around.

It wasn't to be. Yes, we led our division at 24–6. Yes, the fans were excited at our playoff prospects. And yes, we went out in the first round again in three games, this time to the Toronto Blizzard.

And that was it. The Whitecaps were no more. No more struggles, no more triumphs, just a sad, poorly attended little auction to sell off team memorabilia, where Pam Glass, who supervised our press box, shelled out her own money to buy our major trophies and donate them to the BC Sports Hall of Fame because she felt they and the memories should live on and be shared.

There was one personal postscript.

A few days after the team folded, Capozzi called me to his downtown office and asked me how interested I was in politics.

"Not a lot," I said. "Not up to speed on them. More of a distant observer. Why?"

"Well," he said, "I've been asked by the Social Credit Party to see if you'll run in Vancouver East."

It floored me, but I didn't say no right off. I was out of a job and had a family to support.

"But," I protested weakly, "I don't *know anything* about politics."

"No problem," he assured me cheerfully. "We'll give you a crash course. You'll be fine."

I knew what they were thinking. My family lived in Vancouver East and I was a familiar face, but I also knew that it was a locked-in NDP stronghold.

"Well, yes," Capozzi admitted. "But you don't need to *win*. They just want to close the gap."

I talked it over with Deanne, but not too seriously. I was a soccer player and I'd just been through one lost cause. To hell with it.

I'd had a call from Bob McNab asking if I'd like to come to Tacoma and try another shot at indoor soccer. Well, it beat hell out of running for office.

"I'm there," I said, and closed the book—or so I thought—on the Vancouver Whitecaps.

9

THE INCREDIBLE NEWFIES

*"The Honduran delegation unrolled a map of
Canada, looking for St. John's. The more they
unrolled, the bigger their eyes got. How big was
Canada, anyway, and why did they have to play at
one end of it?"*

—Tony Waiters

In 1985 the Canadian Soccer Association launched its bid to get
to the 1986 World Cup final round. There were a few problems:
Canada had no team, no national league and no professional clubs
from which to form its team and—oh, yes—no money. Other than
that, we were in great shape.

Some of those who tried out for the side stayed match fit playing
indoor soccer or on local club sides. Those who were good enough
and lucky enough to catch on with international sides were scattered
all over the globe, playing for teams that grudgingly gave them time
off to compete for their country only because FIFA rules said they
had to. The teams cut that away time to the minimum, often with
dark warnings that there'd be no guarantee their jobs would be there
for them when they returned.

Yes, other countries faced the same restrictions, but they had national leagues in place. The countries Canada would face didn't have many players competing out of country. Mostly they were stay-at-home teams competing with and against each other in league competitions that, given the Central American climate, lasted most of the year. Getting to their national team training mainly involved jumping into their cars or the local transit system.

We did have a coach. Tony Waiters, having risen to what he called "the dizzying heights" of president and general manager of the Whitecaps, decided that being stuck in an office handling paperwork didn't suit him. He'd been offered the national team coaching job in 1977 and had turned it down after a check of the atlas showed him a country that went on forever, meaning its players would be scattered far and wide. Five years later the offer was made again and this time, thankfully, he said yes.

I doubt whether, at the time, he truly realized the scope of the job or the realities he would have to overcome in preparing for the World Cup run two years later. It wasn't so much a lack of player talent—the NASL had just folded and the Canadian players coming home were still in reasonable shape—but keeping together what was essentially a team-in-being until the shooting started with little or nothing in the CSA pot was something else.

Fortunately, Molson Brewery, the national team sponsor, agreed that some of the sponsorship dollars could be spent on player salaries. Tony patched his side together with spit and baling wire, often at the mercy of airline schedules as some of his players, bleary-eyed and bone-weary, yawned their way in from their club sides. Somehow, out of the chaos, he put together a side so special—not so much in ability as in desire and spirit—that even we didn't realize it until that magical September when we fashioned a miracle.

I'm still not sure where the travel money came from, but once Tony had got some idea of the people who might form his World Cup side we hit the road for twenty-one friendly matches around much of the world, trying to get ready for World Cup competition that wouldn't start for eighteen months.

Our 1983 schedule started with a three-game series at home in June against Scotland, which we lost by a combined score of 7–0. In December we regrouped, flew to Mexico and got our asses handed to us, 5–0; we moved on to Honduras and lost twice, 3–1 and 1–0. The second year under Tony didn't go much better. There was a 1–0 road win against Haiti, a 2–0 defeat by Italy in Toronto and a scoreless draw against Chile in Edmonton. Then we were back on the plane to lose 1–0 in Algiers, 2–0 in Tunisia and 3–2 in Morocco, before playing to a scoreless draw in Cyprus and finishing with a 1–0 loss in Cairo. I say "we" loosely. I didn't make that trip (the Whitecaps had folded and I was jobless until catching on with Tacoma to play indoor) but even from a distance it hurt.

What hardly anyone seemed to notice—and who could blame them, given the results?—was that we were starting to come together. The thing was, we knew we had to start proving it.

In 1985 we turned a corner. We beat Trinidad & Tobago 2–1 in Port of Spain, tied Jamaica 1–1 in Montego Bay and played them scoreless in Kingston, lost 1–0 and tied 0–0 vs. Costa Rica on their home turf in San Jose, came home to beat the US 2–0 in Vancouver and then tied them 1–1 in Portland.

Then, just like that, we were playing for keeps in the World Cup elimination rounds, home and home showdowns against CONCACAF countries where soccer was more than just a game to be played and loved—it was *life*!

We got an early break when Jamaica withdrew, moving us along a notch into the second round against Haiti and Guatemala, and another when we got to open both series at home, in Victoria. The Haitians fell 2–0, the Guatemalans 2–1, boosting our confidence for the road rematches, which worked out just fine. We got the draw we needed, 1–1, in Guatemala City and shut out the Haitians 2–0 again in Port au Prince.

Flying home, we tried not to look too far ahead, but the facts hung out there and wouldn't go away: the next round, against

Honduras and Costa Rica, was the last hurdle between us and a trip to the World Cup. We'd had the win and the draw in Costa Rica—friendlies, sure, and their lineup would no doubt be stronger, but we'd handled them. Honduras was a different kettle of fish. We were winless in our last four meetings and some of our veterans, including me, had been there for every loss.

Well, that was one way of looking at it. On the other hand, we were a better team now, two of the four losses had been by one goal, and both John Catliff and George Pakos had scored against them, so they weren't invincible. Yes, the last two losses had come in the past year, but who gave a damn about losses in 1980 and '81? Look at it that way and we were only 0–2. On paper we'd be underdogs, sure, but you know what puppies do on paper. Besides, we had almost three months to get ready. Bring it on!

Of course, individual player commitments got in the way. In two months we managed two matches, both in Korea in something called the President's Cup, which was little more than an exhibition swing. Tony was so excited about it he didn't make the trip. Instead, Bruce Wilson became our temporary playing coach. We lost 2–1 to Ghana, got slapped around 6–1 by Iraq and crept home for the five-week wait for the first showdown with Costa Rica.

We opened at home and managed a 1–1 draw on a goal by Paul James, a disappointment considering how important it was at this level to win on your own turf. A week later we were standing on the pitch in Tegucigalpa, melting in the sweltering Honduran heat and trying to ignore the hostility of 55,000 fans. And here came Pakos, subbing in for Catliff to knock the Honduran monkey off Canada's back with the game's only goal.

Nobody gave any thought to the idea that the goal might be an omen. As it turned out, maybe we should have, but all we cared about was that we had three points—two for the win, one for the draw—out of our first two games. If we could go into San Jose and beat Costa Rica . . .

We couldn't. We drew again, scoreless this time, but Costa Rica had its troubles against the Hondurans, and as it turned out we went into our last match in St. John's knowing that our ticket to Mexico was there for the taking—*IF* we could beat or draw against Honduras. History said that was one hell of an *IF*.

Go ahead: ask. Why St. John's? Everyone else did, including the Hondurans, who got all big-eyed and incredulous when they unrolled their map. (When they arrived on a Thursday for the Saturday match they spent the entire first day in their hotel without setting even a foot outdoors into what they viewed as cold, blustery weather.) The fact was, the Newfoundland Soccer Association had made guarantees for a sellout match no matter who it was against or whether it would turn out to be of any consequence in the qualifying, so the CSA agreed. As Tony said later, "a great move, but purely by chance."

Let me set the stage:

Picture a 7,500-seat stadium by a lake with a graveyard by each of the roads that wound past either side. "Mount Carmel, the Roman Catholic cemetery," a local explains to the media. "And the other one."

"What's *its* name?" someone asks.

"Anglican," the guy says. "Don't know the name and don't care. Doesn't matter anyway because we're goin' up and they're stayin'."

From field level or from one of the bleacher benches that make up the stands you can see a collection of low, grey buildings with walls around them. Lakeside Hotel, the locals called it, otherwise known as Her Majesty's Prison. A block away, an apartment building overlooks the prison yard, the nurses' residence for the local hospital. "The boys in the yard can look up there," the guy chuckles, "and remember what they're missin'."

The media are assured that the place will be jammed at game time despite the local fit of depression caused by a beer strike now in its sixth month, depriving residents of the local brews (including Molson's) and forcing them to consume only imported American brands that, he insists, all taste like they've been distilled through a horse. But they'll be out in numbers on the big day.

"This isn't a village on the ass end of nowhere, y'know," he adds proudly. "We've got restaurants as good as anywhere. We've even got a gay bar. It's called Strangers. It used to be called Friends and now it's called Strangers, and y'can make of that what y'will."

Media types reluctantly leave this gold mine of information, their atmosphere stories already written in their minds, and head in to inspect the stadium.

The pitch itself is decent enough, and the wind has died down to gusts, which may explain why, during our first workout, only two balls sail over one goal and into Quidi Vidi Lake about 100 feet beyond the park. "If you win the toss, take the wind and press like hell," the locals urge Waiters. "Then pray it changes or dies at intermission." It's a mild source of concern because the Hondurans like to play the ball on the carpet and a lot of our

Carl Valentine (seen here out-leaping Toronto's Colin Franks) arrived from Manchester with jetpack speed and a love for the game and for the city of Vancouver that soon led to Canadian citizenship and a spot on our World Cup team in '86. KENT KALLBERG

attack is based on the long ball, but as Bruce said at the team meeting, "We're here and we control our own destiny. Can't ask for more than that."

Our big worry, though, was the state of our roster. Two starters, central defender Terry Moore and midfielder Mike Sweeney, were sitting out suspensions. Gerry Gray's match fitness was in question. Tony sent out an emergency call to Carl Valentine at West Albion. Carl was eligible because he'd taken out his Canadian citizenship in the Whitecap days and had never committed to any other country for World Cup completion. He arrived on the Tuesday before match day—sick as a dog. Perfect. We kept the state of his health a secret. "I'll be there," he wheezed, and somehow convinced Tony he was fit enough to start. Thank heaven.

I can't say enough good things about the spirit and generosity of the St. John's people. Consider what happened about twenty minutes before kickoff.

The stadium was jammed. Suddenly the buzz was interrupted by the sound of music. Out of nowhere, a band of Hondurans—estimates later ranged from 100 to 300—are at the gates. They have no tickets. There's not a seat visible, but St. John's was equal to the challenge.

"We have guests," says the man on the PA system. "Would y'all be sliding over a bit so we can welcome them in."

Room was made. The Honduran fans sat down and, surrounded by locals, began to cheer for their team. Name me one other place in Canada where that could have happened. But they were soccer fans, and in St. John's that was enough. (Other Honduran fans weren't as lucky. When they booked their flights to Canada they booked for Saint John, not St. John's. They landed in New Brunswick, couldn't get another flight in time and wound up watching the game on TV in a bar.)

The Honduran side weren't nearly as jolly. They didn't like the size of the pitch or the goalposts and even brought in a FIFA referee to measure everything. Their confidence, however, bordered on arrogance. "The Canadians caught us by surprise (in the 1–0 loss in

Honduras)," said Porfirio Betancourt. "We just had a bad day, which we will correct on Saturday."

Sure.

Here's the thing about big games: you're so busy doing your thing that you don't always see the whole picture. That comes later when you have time to reflect, or when you get home and check the local media reports. The report in the *Vancouver Province* the morning after seemed to say it all:

> St. John's, Nfld. — Hello, Victoria? Listen, if your water meters break down next summer, don't expect George Pakos to fix them. George is going to Mexico City. Hello, Honduras? Tell the guy who distributes those T-shirts, the ones with the faces of the Honduran and Costa Rican coaches on the front over the message "Which One to Mexico?" that he backed the wrong face. Tony Waiters says thanks for the shirt and it will look good on his wall, but he's the one who's going to Mexico, as coach of the unlikeliest bunch of heroes Canada has ever produced.
>
> Hello, Mr. Guinness? Get ready for an insert. Your book can't come out without this.
>
> Start with the fact that Team Canada knocked off Honduras 2–1 here yesterday to become Canada's first team ever to reach the final round of the World Cup, the biggest soccer show—hell, the biggest sports show—of them all, next summer in Mexico City. Throw in that they did it in St. John's, Newfoundland, the oldest town in the country, where the sceptics who said it couldn't and shouldn't be done measured the size of the stadium but forgot to measure the boundless capacity of the Newfie heart.
>
> Make a note, please, that these people on the edge of nowhere made it sound like BC Place Stadium, and

the players had only to look up to a sea of Canadian flags and hear "Na Na, Hey Hey, Kiss 'em Goodbye" to gather strength when things got tough.

You shoulda been there, Mr. Guinness. You'd love this team.

Start with Carl Valentine, an English kid who got his Canadian citizenship in April 1984 and flew in from West Bromwich last Tuesday as an emergency replacement at forward. Sick all week, he was, although they kept it semi-secret, but he laid out two perfect corners to set up a goal in each half and got the full-court press that is the Canadian game established early.

How sick? "He was breathing out his arse when I took him out (late in the game)" Waiters said. "But that was better than what he'd been doing with it all week."

The first goal was scored by Pakos, who had the only goal in the first meeting with Honduras. Pursuit of the World Cup berth has cost him five leaves-of-absence without pay from his water meter repair job in Victoria. At thirty-three you might think the game is behind him, but don't tell his teammates, who were pouring beer over him in the dressing room and singing "One Georgie Pakos! There's only one Georgie Pakos!" to the tune of "Guantanamera."

The other goal came from the wonderfully named Igor Vrablic on a flick-on from Bob Lenarduzzi off Valentine's corner. Waiters held a secret pre-practice workout Friday to perfect that set play and they ran it as he drew it. "Igor! Igor!" the crowd shouted. Igor ran his usual 10,000 miles with his usual disregard for life, limb or obstacle, then retired to the lab for another jolt of electricity.

Oh, yes—over here we have Randy Samuel, the Trinidad-born youngster pressed into service on the back line by the suspension to Terry Moore. The play he made late in the first half, Mr. Guinness, deserves at least a page.

Goalie Tino Lettieri (Have I told you about his stuffed parrot, Ozzie? Never mind.) had a ball drift over his head. It was rolling toward the empty net, inches from the line, with Figuero of Honduras in hot pursuit for a goal that could have been a backbreaker. Out of nowhere came Samuel, throwing himself through the dirt to hook it away with inches to spare.

"I was three steps behind Figuero," he said later. "All I was trying to do was catch up, maybe bother him so he'd blow the shot. But I got a foot on it, and when the ball went up it hit his arm and bounced clear. If it had hit his body, it was in."

There are so many great stories on this team, you see—people like Lenarduzzi and Bruce Wilson, who've been there forever and have lived through the birth and death of the professional game in Canada and now, at last, get a chance to play in the greatest showpiece of them all. And kids like Samuel and Vrablic, and a vet like Pakos, who wistfully wondered after the match if next summer he might get time off with pay to represent his country, which would make it easier on the wife and kids.

This team has been ignored in its own country, refused financial aid by its government and kept alive through the courtesy of Molson's brewery and the willingness of soccer people to budget for a $275,000 deficit and pray for a miracle.

It wasn't supposed to get this far. It wasn't supposed to go to Central America and beat Honduras and draw with Costa Rica. "A mistake," the Honduran players said of the 1–0 loss. "We will correct it."

Yesterday, they got their chance—and Canada got its miracle.

> Team Canada is going to Mexico. If you need a cat-
> egory, Mr. Guinness, try "Biggest Hearts, One Team."

More than a touch of homerism there—but why not? In six months, Canada was going to the World Cup!

In real life, not all fairy tales have happy endings. Sometimes the wolf really does eat Little Red Riding Hood, the hare beats the tortoise and the three little pigs don't get into the brick house in time and wind up as one layer of a BLT. In our hearts we probably knew that, but we'd had such a great qualification run, the Newfoundland experience had been such an incredible high, that we dared to dream. Not of winning the World Cup or even coming close—just of doing well, perhaps even reaching the second round.

Our roster as we entered the final sixteen is worth noting because, among other things, it shows the vast difference between us

This was the starting lineup for the Newfoundland match vs. Honduras, where victory punched Canada's ticket for the 1986 World Cup competition in Mexico City. With me in the back row (L to R): Randy Ragan, Randy Samuel, Ian Bridge, Igor Vrablic, George Pakos. Front: Carl Valentine, Paul James, Tino Lettieri, Bruce Wilson, David Norman. LENARDUZZI COLLECTION and teams from countries where the game was historically rooted. Under the Club section of the official lineups, for six of our twenty-two-man squad—defenders Bruce Wilson (our captain, for Pete's sake) and Randy Samuel (whose heroics played such a big part in getting us there), midfielders Randy Ragan, Greg Ion and Jamie Lowery and reserve keeper Sven Habermann—it said "No club."

Dale Mitchell, David Norman and I were playing indoor soccer in Tacoma to make a few bucks and mainly to stay as sharp and in as good a shape as possible. Lettieri was doing the same thing in Minnesota, Valentine, Mike Sweeney and Pasquale De Luca in Cleveland, Gerry Gray in Chicago, Branco Segota in San Diego and Paul Dolan in Edmonton. Pakos was back at work in Victoria and playing for the Victoria Athletic Association.

Terry Moore came in from Glentoran in Belfast, Ian Bridge from La Chaux-de-Fonds in Switzerland, Igor Vrablic from Seraing in Belgium, Colin Miller from the Glasgow Rangers. Paul James had no travel worries. He'd been playing with CF Monterrey in Mexico.

You think the playing pedigree of that lineup sent shivers up other World Cup spines? Somehow, I doubted it.

The draw had been held around Christmas and we were in against France, fourth-place finishers in the '82 event, the Soviet Union and Hungary. I could rattle off the names of every player on the French side and be in awe of all of them. Russia was rated a strong contender. Hungary was given only an outside chance but, although we didn't know much about their players, we'd been hearing ominous things about their performance of late.

I watched the draw on CBC television and saw at once that we were in tough. Then again, being realistic, we'd have been in tough against anybody, and so what? We were going to play in the *World Cup finals*. Tough draw or no tough draw, we'd be *there*.

My only regret was that the thing would be played in Mexico. Nothing against the country or the people, who were kind, generous and hospitable, but we'd played there in qualifying rounds and assorted other competitions for years. If we were going to play on the world stage, why did it have to be that part of the world? Brazil, maybe, or France or anywhere else in Europe, preferably somewhere where the altitude didn't suck the oxygen from your lungs and turn your legs to rubber.

The altitude has always been Mexico's edge—that and the fact that somehow international games are always scheduled around noon when the vehicular traffic makes the gas fumes so thick you can almost taste them. It takes ten to fourteen days to adjust to high altitudes. Club teams usually arrived two days early at best, which was like telling the Mexican sides to loaf through the first half because they'd be able to score at will in the second while the visitors gasped like fish flopping on a riverbank.

There was also the matter of the psychological warfare. To get to the 120,000-seat Estadio Azteca the visiting team's bus had to creep down *Blvd. de Muerto*—the Boulevard of Death—so named, we were told, because "many people died in battle here in olden times, and it's said that sometimes you can hear the screams of the ghosts." It was a slow trip due to the fans swarming on both sides of the road, holding up fingers so our players would know how many goals we were going to give up and how many we'd score. For our game against France they needed two hands—eight or nine fingers for France and then a circle of thumb and forefinger for Canada while the other hand made the throat-slitting motion accompanied by cries of "Canada! You gonna *die*!"

In terms of playing at altitude, we had no excuses. We'd trained in Colorado for two to three weeks, depending upon individual club or indoor soccer commitments. We were as ready as we could be, but no amount of physical and mental readiness could overcome the opening-game awe as we stood in the tunnel right next to our captain, Bruce Wilson . . . That was *Michel Platini* actually speaking to Bruce and saying he recognized him, probably from the time Platini's touring Juventus club played the Blizzard in Toronto.

We knew what we had to do against France: play scared, not in the fear sense but in the "take-no-chances, think defence first and look for the counter" sense. So we went out and for twenty minutes we got absolutely pummelled, and on one play at least we should have been down a goal.

I was chasing back toward our goal for a ball that had been played behind me to a man on my goal side, at a bit of an angle but inside the box. He was smart. He just stopped dead, I bowled him over and he went down in a heap. The ref was behind me. I fell myself, rolled over and looked back, praying I wouldn't see the whistle in his mouth. I didn't, and I still don't know why, because he should have been putting the ball on the spot for a penalty. But, hey, it was France, and it was still scoreless.

We had what everyone watching the telecast in Canada and even the announcer thought was a great chance, a free kick from Mike Sweeney that Ian Bridge headed past the post—*wide* past the post. The TV camera angle made it look like the ball had actually hit the post and that's how the announcer called it. "Canada has hit the post!" Not even close.

We kept it scoreless until the 81-minute mark, when Paul Dolan (who got the start in goal because Tino's indoor soccer commitments hadn't given him enough training time) and I got our wires crossed. The ball came hanging high at the far post. I was on the line and thought Doley was going to get it. He missed it, but no problem. It was going to go over the line for a goal kick. Except that it didn't. Somehow their winger got behind me and headed it into the goalmouth. Jean-Pierre Papin rose to meet it, nodded it in, and we lost 1–0.

There was a funny finale. As the clock wound down to the final minute, a lot of our guys seemed to be hanging around Platini. They weren't marking him, they were trying to time it so when the final whistle blew they'd be close enough to ask for his jersey, not knowing they were already too late. David Norman had asked Platini for the jersey with about ten minutes left in the game. Platini had said okay, he'd trade in the tunnel after the match, which they did. Naturally, David got a lot of stick from the rest of us about it afterward. No doubt some of it was jealousy. David's still got it. Makes you wonder, doesn't it, whether Platini still has David's.

In retrospect, the narrow loss to France did more damage than the loss of potential points. In the game after ours, Russia absolutely *hammered* Hungary 6–0. The Hungarians looked like they were running in sand.

Well now, we lose one-nil to France and Hungary gets smoked 6–0 by Russia? We've got the Hungarians next. Hell, we should be fine. So, instead of staying with the play-scared strategy that had worked so well against France, we went out and played like we were the bloody favourites. We lost 2–0 in a game that was there for us to win.

We'd had a bit of a goalie controversy. Tino had proclaimed himself ready and, as the guy who'd been in the nets through our qualifying matches, probably deserved to start. Certainly he couldn't be faulted on either of the two goals, but Doley had played really well against France and there was some thought, heading into our last qualifying-round match against the Russians, that maybe he should get the start.

Canada vs. France, our first World Cup match in '86, which we lost 1-0. Back row (L to R): Me, Ian Bridge, Paul Dolan, Igor Vrablic, Randy Samuel, Randy Ragan. Front: Dave Norman, Bruce Wilson, Carl Valentine, Paul James, Mike Sweeney. LENARDUZZI COLLECTION

Never got to win it, but at least I got to hold it: the most coveted sports trophy on the planet, the FIFA World Cup. LENARDUZZI COLLECTION

We weren't going to advance, we knew that, but there was another issue. The bookmakers were giving odds—big odds—that Canada would go through the tournament without scoring a goal. The game was being televised back to Canada. We couldn't get shut out again. We went out against the Russians determined to go out with guns blazing. Never mind how many goals they got, we had to get at least one.

Tino started, we lost 2–0, and I became the answer to a trivia question: Who was the Canadian who missed a sure chance to score?

Guilty.

With about ten minutes to play I was at my usual spot at the far post looking to flick on. The ball went over my head. I turned around, a couple of guys went up for it, and damned if it didn't come to me just inside the six-yard box. It hit me, fell to the ground, and if I knew one thing for sure it was that I had to get the shot away quickly because inside the six-yard box there'd be someone tackling or the goalie rushing out to block it.

One problem: the ball was on my left foot, not my preferred right one, and there was no time to switch. I rushed the shot, stubbed my toe, got mostly turf and watched the ball dribble towards the net. When I saw the replay there was one small comfort: The goalie had dived to stop the ball. He didn't have to. He could have just kicked it away, no problem, but it made it look like a good save on what must have been a decent shot, when it was neither.

Being a trivia answer is a kind of immortality, I guess. *Nineteen years* later, Jim Taylor was picking up his tickets at Will Call for a match at West Ham. One of the ushers saw his Canada badge and opened the conversation with "Canadian? You guys had that guy in the World Cup in Mexico—Lenar-something?"

"Lenarduzzi," he was told.

"Yeah, that's him," he snorted. "Missed a sitter, 'e did. A fookin' *sitter*."

Oh, one last thing: Nobody at home saw it live on TV. The telecast of the country's national team playing its last game at its first-ever World Cup final was pre-empted.

By *Sesame Street*.

10

HANGIN' 'EM UP

"Enjoy your playing days, because nothing you do
afterwards is going to be anywhere near as enjoyable."
—Alan Hinton, 1978

I was thirty-one years old and out of work. From age fourteen, the only paying job I'd ever had involved kicking a ball or stopping other people from kicking it. Now I'd found work trying to convince people they should buy season tickets for a team that didn't yet exist.

Tony Waiters had broached the subject when we were in Mexico at the World Cup. The CSA was forming a new league to open in the summer of '87. Would I be interested in (a) playing for and coaching a Vancouver side and (b) being, in effect, the face of the franchise during the formation process, drumming up the interest and getting people to put their money down for seats they wouldn't be using for a year?

An office job? Me? Regular hours, a *desk* and maybe even, God forbid, a suit and tie? On the other hand, I *was* out of work. It might be nice to have a few bucks coming in for a few months. The idea of being a playing coach was intriguing, and if the coaching thing didn't work out, I'd just play. Yeah, I was interested.

"Good," he said, and when we got back to Vancouver I jumped into the deep end of the pool.

What with the millions invested in today's MLS franchise and the 15,000-plus season ticket pledges, it's strange in a way to recall that this whole thing began with me out there in pubs, speaking to small gatherings organized by the new club's directors.

"Hi. I'm Bobby Lenarduzzi. We're just back from the World Cup, we want to help to make sure we can grow and continue to qualify for World Cups to come, so we've got this new team we're calling the Vancouver '86ers because it was formed this year and one hundred years ago in 1886 the city of Vancouver was incorporated, and how about supporting us by buying season tickets?"

I was essentially selling one ticket at a time, two if we were lucky and the guy had a wife or a kid who played the game.

I was flying by the seat of my pants, going into an office where there was no one to talk to or ask questions as I tried to think about putting together a team, and hitting the pubs at night to talk soccer to people I had to sell on the idea of committing money to a new league when the last one, the NASL, had died such a mournful death.

It was an eye-opener. Being a player at the professional or national level meant that all you had to do, aside from playing and training to play, was show up. Everything was laid out for you when you arrived. You put on the boots, strip or sweats, and went out and kicked the ball. On road trips you were checked in when you got to the airport, the PR man handed you your boarding pass and away you went. When you got to the hotel nobody asked you to register because that had been done in advance, too. Somebody handed you your key and you were in. Lining up to check in was for ordinary folks. You were a *professional footballer*.

I really had no idea what to do. I'd never been in an office environment, and I had some evidence that I wasn't cut out for it. When Adidas had an opening for a Vancouver sales rep I was interviewed by a nice guy named Gerry Fisher, who asked me questions about how I'd handle the business side. I answered as best I could, considering that I had absolutely no idea. Years later, I met Gerry again and joked that it was a good thing he hadn't given me that job. He smiled and said, "I think you're in the right place." Translation: he'd have had to tell me I wasn't suitable for the job, and I don't think he'd wanted to.

There were lessons for me everywhere, including one from Alan Hinton the day my initial gut reaction was that he was a prick.

That summer I'd gone to Tacoma to play indoor soccer. Hinton, my '78 teammate and the guy whose pinpoint passes on set plays had played a key role in that player-of-the-year award, was now my head coach. Midway through training camp, he called me into his office. "Bob, there's no easy way to do this. We're going to let you go."

"Okay," I said, and left. Fortunately, I hadn't changed into my gear yet, so I didn't have to take it off and get back into civvies. Players commiserated with me, and I walked out. By now I'm thinking: "What an a-hole! Couldn't he have said something more, dressed it up a little, talked about the career I'd had and how sorry he was? Jerk!"

However, once I calmed down I realized that he'd done it the right way. If he'd sugar-coated it I'd probably still have thought he was an a-hole for saying nice things and then canning me. Either way, I was going to be upset. When I got into coaching myself, I remembered the experience and used Hinton's approach: Don't beat around the bush. Be respectful, but get it done and don't dwell on it.

By now another old name had surfaced with the '86ers: Buzz Parsons was the first general manager and actually the guy who hired me as playing coach as Tony and I had discussed. Now my job description was more comfortable: Find the players and build a team.

My introduction to the media as playing coach was kind of funny as I told them how I wanted offensive-minded players who'd play aggressive soccer and none of this kicking the ball back to the keeper because it was time-wasting crap and we would damned well entertain people so they'd have a reason to come back. In his *Province* column the next morning, Jim Taylor inserted the needle. "A defender all his life," he marvelled, "and now he wants to think offence?"

Finding players who filled my bill was an education in itself. I think our entire player budget was around $150,000 give or take $30,000. A good player was making $2,000 a month for five months, and we didn't have many who got that much. Those who could play indoor soccer—Valentine was one of them—came directly to us from there and therefore had year-round employment. Others, like Catliff and Paul Dolan with Umbro, held outside jobs while they played. The one common denominator was nobody was getting rich.

Despite this, my problem wasn't finding players—it was sorting through the ones who showed up. Our open tryout camps drew guys from all over North America, including one from Philadelphia who was so out of his depth he should have worn scuba gear. He really wanted to play, so he'd flown in to bust his butt trying for a job that would pay him barely enough in a month to cover his air fare. I really hated to tell him he had no future in the game, but I did.

"Thanks for the advice, coach," he said, "and thanks for your honesty. But I'll keep looking." And away he went, looking for another place—any place—to pursue his dream.

You never know, though, when you might strike gold.

Early in the search process I would get excited when people from all over Europe and Central America phoned me to say, "Boy, have I got a player for *you!*" I soon realized that they were representing a bunch of self-proclaimed phenoms whose attitude was "Hey, I'm from Brazil and that's Canada. I might be able to play there even if I'm not very good, because they don't play real soccer over there." They were crap, but thought we were worse than crap.

So when a man from the local Fijian community approached to say he had a player for me and I should bring him in because he'd be a big attraction for the people from his homeland, I wasn't all that impressed.

"No, no," he insisted. "He plays for the Fijian national team. Bring him in—and if he doesn't make it, no hard feelings." And that's how we found Ivor Evans, who stayed for ten seasons.

Ivor impressed me from the moment he got here, and won his spot in a pre-season tournament in Kelowna, where we went up against a Calgary side that featured right back Burke Kaiser, a starter for Canada's under-20 team. Ivor turned him inside out. He was just the kind we were looking for, a player with speed and flair who could go around people and create instant excitement. He was also one tough s.o.b.

There came a game in which Catliff got on Ivor's case and just wouldn't let up. Nothing personal, that was just John, so intensely competitive and with such a burning desire to win that he pushed his teammates as hard as he pushed himself. But Ivor wasn't about to hold still for it. At the next training session, he politely asked me if he could have a moment.

"You have to tell John to shut up," he said. "Because if he doesn't, I am going to beat him up."

Now John stood 6'1", a tough, mean and raw-boned guy who could leap high enough to give defenders nosebleeds and landed in a bad mood with elbows flying. Ivor was short and stocky and quiet, but it never occurred to me that he was bluffing or would fail to give a good account of himself should the two ever have it out. Fortunately, it never came to that—but I'd have paid to see it.

Catliff was a piece of work, a Harvard grad who played like a street kid. In practice you hated to play with him, but in games you loved to (even if he did rake you unmercifully when you made a mistake) because he was such a winner. He was also the guy who created a pivotal moment in my young coaching career.

I was in my second year. Having spent the first season in Calgary, John was now an '86er and his impact was huge, but there came a game where he had the worst half I'd ever seen him play.

As the coach, it was my job to tell him so, just as I would any other player, but to tell the truth, that Harvard education thing had always intimidated me, maybe because I was so conscious of not finishing my own Grade 12. So what I say to him, in front of everyone, was "John! We need more from you!"

And he looks at me and says, "Can you be more specific?"

In my mind, I was rooted there in silence for two or three minutes. Normally, when you go after a guy, he says "Yeah, okay. I'll do better," but here was this really educated guy quietly asking me for specifics.

I took a deep breath.

"Yeah," I said. "I can, actually. Your first touch is crap, you're not closing down when you don't have the ball and you're not winning anything in the air. Is that enough for you?"

"Yes," he said, and it was a very meek yes.

Internally, I heaved a monumental sigh, because we were there in the change room where everyone had heard the exchange. I honestly think that if I'd been hesitant or stumbled, it could have been a very bad moment for me. It's like teachers say: Establish your control early. If you don't, it will be a l-o-n-g, l-o-n-g year.

Coaching always was a learning experience, as management is now and ever will be. Starting out as a player-coach made it even more difficult, because there were times when one got in the way of the other. My answer, and not a wise one, was to become a real live "Roy of the Rovers." He was a cartoon character in England who does everything—scores, passes, dribbles through the whole team, *everything*, so when English fans saw a guy trying to be the whole show, they'd dub him Roy of the Rovers.

That first season, that was me. As a player I took every throw-in, every free kick, while simultaneously trying to coach everyone else, hammering my guys for not doing what they were supposed to be doing. Result: I wasn't totally focused on either side of what had become a soccer split personality.

Still, it was a fine first season and got off to a dynamite start. As part of the ticket drive we'd obtained the old Whitecaps' season ticket list, which contained about 12,000 names. We contacted them all and convinced about 2,500 of them that they should give the pro game a second chance. And then we signed Carl Valentine.

Everybody loved Carl. They still do. When we brought him into the MLS organization last year, my telephone, fax and e-mail went crazy as people let me know what a great idea it was. He'd been such a class act throughout his career here, and no one who was in the streets for the victory parade in 1979 would ever forget him standing there in a white suit, puffing a big black cigar and shouting: "You are the No. 1 fans, and we are the No. 1 team!"

No one was happier than I was to see him back. In 1999, in the crazy way this game works out, I'd been the guy who'd had to fire him.

Carl had taken over as Whitecaps coach when I left to coach the nationals, so short of players that he'd suited up again himself in an effort to provide on-field leadership. When I got back, now as general manager, the club was coming off a string of poor seasons and we needed to make a coaching change.

Rather than calling him into the office and him having to walk out through the building without a job, a feeling I knew from getting sacked as an indoor player in Tacoma, I met him at a Starbucks and gave him the bad news. He took it professionally, as I knew he would, because Carl would always be Carl. In the years that followed he never uttered a bad word about the firing to anyone—and in a community as tight and gossipy as soccer's, believe me, if he had said anything it would have gotten back to me. So, bringing him back into the organization was a pure joy. It's been as though no time has passed since that opening day . . .

So, we had a 3,500 season ticket base in 4,200-seat Swangard, and on opening night, June 7, 1987, we jammed in 7,000 in a standing-room-only welcome back for the game and, in no small part, for Carl.

I was still into my "excitement first" pitch with the players, in the belief that if we played to a scoreless draw a whole bunch of customers wouldn't be back. A composite of the million or so times I tried to beat it into them would go something like this:

"Don't pass the ball back to the keeper from the halfway line. I know it's safe, but it sucks. Try to turn it outside. Maybe it will turn into a great play for us, maybe you'll get stripped and the other guys will score. If they do, I'll put my hand up after the game and tell the media I told you to do it.

"When the ball goes out of play on the sideline, don't feel you have to take a minute or so to get it back in. When I sit in the stands and see that, it drives me crazy. Show some urgency! Run over the line, get the ball from the ballboy and fire it in! Let's have the fans feel like we're really trying to play a high-speed game. Some things you can't control, but these you can, so do it.

"Ivor, you dive. Do it on this team and your next dive will be off the bench. You go down like you've been shot and in a minute you're up and running? People *hate* that."

See, even back then I thought that our game needed a wake-up call, and I think it's even more evident now. Maybe the rest of the world is okay with it, because everywhere else the game is played the attitude is the one Canadians have for hockey: We may bitch about it, but we'll watch, no matter what. However, even in some of those countries attendance is declining, and FIFA is so conservative that major change would require a massive attitude switch.

The first thing I'd do is put in an over-and-back rule. Once the ball is over the centre line, if you pass it back over it again into your half of the field, it's an automatic free kick for the other team. Right now teams can, and do, pass it all the way back to the goalie. You can kill the game within the rules. Make that one change and as a defender I know I can come and get you once you leave your half, because you can't just pull that chicken switch and pound it back into your zone.

While we're at it, let's bring back the NASL's 35-yard offside line. Georgio Chinaglia made a living at the 35. You couldn't leave him there, you had to cover him, and that opened space. Coaches can clutter today's game to death. Let's give the creative players some room.

And on, and on, and on . . . Maybe I was still high from the week's big event at practice, when a policeman came to tell me that Deanne had gone into labour and was on her way to hospital to deliver our second child—any excuse in a storm—but one thing I did get right on opening night, and the fates rewarded us with a miracle. As Carl was warming up I took him aside and said:

"Because of who you are and the reception you're going to get when you take the field, if you happen to score, and the goal is a good one, I want you to turn and run full speed to the crowd and make them feel a part of it."

I don't know why I said it. It was as though I felt I had to script the game. Carl was fast and exciting, but he'd never been a big goal scorer. Anyway, about seventeen minutes into the scoreless game he lets go a rocket into the top corner, runs to the stands and throws himself at the crowd. Brilliant! Cecil B. Lenarduzzi strikes again! We go on to win 4–2 and the crowd goes nuts. For me, it couldn't have been more perfect: the birth of my daughter and the rebirth of the Whitecaps. (We christened her Sunny, which she's been to this day.)

However, for every up, there's a down. I was trying to find my way as coach, and the results weren't always encouraging. Nobody suffered from that inconsistency more than Dominic Mobilio.

Poor Dom. I was so hard on him, and he was seventeen. I yelled at him so much, for what I thought were all the right reasons, trying to make him a better player and maybe expecting too much. He must have felt like he could do nothing right, because I was on him even when he made the right play. Once he had the ball in the middle of the park, didn't know what to do with it, hesitated for a minute and then had the ball stripped away. And I yelled at him again.

I wasn't aware of it. But at the end of the season our trainer, Lou Moro, took me aside.

"I need to tell you something," he said. "You've got Dom running in circles. He doesn't know *what* you want. You tell him one thing, he does it and you yell at him. He does another, you yell at him again. You've got to let up on him and let him *play*."

It was like having an ice bucket dumped on me, because right away I knew he was right. I was so wound up being a player-coach that I was doing things I shouldn't have been doing, but good old Lou, he let me know. All I could say was "Thank you."

That conversation was one of the things that spurred me into some self analysis and a couple of inescapable conclusions, the first being that my determination to play go-go attacking soccer may have cost us a chance to reach the championship game.

We were up 3–1 in the semi-final in Calgary, where we were under no obligation to entertain anybody, but instead of concentrating on holding on to what we had, I had us pressing for a fourth goal. They got one back, tied it late and beat us 4–3 in overtime. I heard later that one of our directors was so upset at what he saw as my lack of focus that he wanted me fired. Who knows where the road might have taken me had the guy gotten his wish? My coaching career might have been over almost before it started. In year two, I'd have to get a better handle on this business of being a player-coach.

I sat down with Alan Errington and said: "Okay, when I'm on the field, you're the coach. Don't be looking out at me to find out if what you're going to do is okay. You make the subs as you see fit," I told him, then grinned and added: "As long as you don't sub me, I'm okay with that."

It worked. I focused on the playing side, still coaching on the field but only in terms of organizing people, talking to them and encouraging them—all things I'd done all my life as a player anyway. With Alan handling the sidelines and seeing things I might not see from the middle of the action, everything simply ran more smoothly and the stress levels dropped for both me and the players—Dominic in particular.

I'd taken him aside when we first began training and apologized for what had happened the previous year.

"I know now that I was too hard on you, and I'm sorry about that," I told him. "I'm not going to stop being constructively critical but I'm going to give you some room." I did, and he was a better player for it.

Before long we were rocketing through a stretch that seemed pre-destined to conclude with a championship, but as the streak went on I began to get the feeling that it was time for Lenarduzzi the coach to retire Lenarduzzi the player. It wasn't that I was playing poorly, but the niggling little injuries I'd somehow avoided for most of my career were beginning to gain on me. The instant post-game bounce-back was taking longer and, in terms of timing, the odds that I could leave on a high note seemed pretty good given the way the side was performing.

I thought it over and then made the official announcement that this would be my final playing season, that henceforth I would con-centrate on coaching.

It caught people by surprise, because I was still playing at a good level. Tony Taylor, getting the national team ready for World Cup qualification rounds, even suggested that there could be a spot for me on the squad, providing some veteran experience on a very young team.

That was momentarily tempting, because I honestly felt I could go on for a couple more seasons. Still, I didn't want to end my career sitting on the bench as the old vet encouraging the kids. "I'd want to come in and compete for a spot, with a decent chance of being a starter," I told him. He couldn't make that commitment, so I de-clined with thanks. Still, it was nice to be asked.

Meanwhile, the '86ers rolled on in the midst of a forty-six-game unbeaten streak (37 wins, 9 draws) that would stretch into the following season, set a record for any professional team in North American sport and put the '89 team that concluded it into the BC Sports Hall of Fame.

First, though, there was the matter of winning the '88 cham-pionship game against the Hamilton Steelers—my last game as a player—in front of the home crowd at Swangard Stadium. What could be sweeter than that, as long as we won? And it honestly never occurred to me that we would not. My big problem, though, was making sure I was *in* it.

In the summer of '88, my body started sending me hints that I wasn't as young as I used to be. With the league title stowed away, I hung up old No. 5 for good. KENT KALLBERG

I'd come with a thigh strain, strapped it up and kept playing, but it was starting to be a problem. Although I didn't broadcast it, I honestly feared I might not be ready, but I was still assuring the media that we'd win. It caused a bit of a media stir, because I'd never before said anything like that going into a game.

"You're predicting you're going to win?" asked TV broadcaster Barry Houlihan.

"Oh, yeah," I said. "There's no way we're going to lose."

What I meant was that, this being my last game as a player, there was no way I was going to finish with a defeat, especially not in front of the home crowd. Still, it came out like a boast, and that upset Steelers' coach John McGrane no end. Naturally, the story wound up on their dressing room wall, one of those time-honoured Knute Rockne type storybook ploys that supposedly lead teams to kick down the dressing room door, rush out onto the pitch and stomp the braggarts into the turf.

So much for storybooks. We beat them 4–1 and hoisted the trophy—and there I was, leaving the field for the last time as a player, a bit melancholy but totally fulfilled.

The big test would come, of course, when the team gathered for next season's training camp. As many a veteran athlete has learned, the time to call it quits isn't at the end of a season—it's at the beginning of the new one when the old competitive juices start flowing again and you start telling yourself that one more season wouldn't hurt. But I knew in my heart it was time. It wasn't as though I was leaving the *game*, I was just moving on to a new phase of it, the full-time business of coaching, and no one in the CSL would have a better core of playing talent than the one with which I'd been blessed. So no looking back. Not yet, anyway. Bring it on.

On the surface, everything was perfect. We had an abundance of playing talent and rode it to four straight league titles before losing it to Winnipeg. Our fans were loyal, our crowds good. We weren't making money, but nor was anyone else, and the losses weren't astronomical: $50,000 to $80,000 in the early going. However, times were changing. The MLS was open for business and that meant competitive employment opportunities, which meant bigger losses as the club shelled out to keep its core players. Sooner or later something had to give—and something did: the entire league collapsed at the end of the '92 season.

Come to think of it, maybe now would be a good point to pause and look at the tangle that was the structure of North American soccer in the 1990s, when leagues came and went and apparently most of them had learned nothing from the debacle of the NASL.

The American Professional Soccer League (APSL) was formed in 1990 out of an amalgamation of something called the Western Soccer League and the American Soccer League (not to be confused with two earlier leagues with the same names that were born and died almost unnoticed). It opened with unbridled optimism and twenty-two franchises. Two years later, it had five and probably would have collapsed if the CSL hadn't beaten it to the graveyard. The '86ers, Toronto Blizzard and Montreal Impact jumped to the APSL, which might have worked out had it not been blind-sided by circumstance.

Remember that condition FIFA put on US Soccer's successful bid to stage the '94 World Cup: that it establish a national professional league? In December of 1993, the APSL, the MLS and League One America all applied to the US Soccer Federation to form that league. No doubt the APSL thought it had a pretty good shot, being the only one of the three actually in operation and with several members of the US national team on its roster, but the well-financed MLS won the day and the APSL was on borrowed time and . . . enough! I'm getting a headache.

The point is that it's not easy to set up and support a professional team, let alone a professional league. It requires dedication, commitment and the knowledge that you're not going to make a lot of (read: any) money, which in turn means you've got to have some special people ready to dig into their own pockets purely out of love for the game.

Take the '86ers. The stake that got them started was raised by eighty-six people, including me, putting up $500 apiece. We had eighty-four, got two more, and decided to cut it off because it tied in nicely with the name. Then we got really lucky. Milan Ilich stepped up when things were getting rocky and took over the franchise. I have never met a more honourable man than Milan, who sealed most of his deals in the construction and development business with nothing more than a handshake. He had the team for ten years, and even when he sold to David Braley he made a $50,000 commitment to the club and bought a bunch of season tickets. It was a pleasure to know him, as it was to work for and with him.

Over the years the club has been blessed with people like Milan who, through love of the game or a simple desire to lend a hand to a community venture, came forward with commitment and support both moral and monetary. I run the risk here of overlooking some, but there are two whom I believe deserve a deep bow.

Wendy McDonald of BC Bearing was an original Whitecaps director. She jokes now that it cost her money to get out, but she was there again recently with a $10,000 donation to the White-caps Foundation. And, speaking of love of the game, how about our long-time radio play-by-play man Ian Michaud, a fan whose twin passions were, and are, opera and Borussia Mönchengladbach of the German Bundesliga. At one of our low points, when there were no funds to meet the payroll, he put up $50,000 of his own money to keep us afloat. He was repaid, but had no certainty that he would be. He was a fan, his club was in trouble, and that was enough.

The only club owner we had who broke that profit jinx was Braley, who took over the franchise in 1997, the year I came back from the national team to become GM and the year the APSL became the A League. Mind you, Mr. Braley had an edge: He also owned the CFL's BC Lions and was able to shift some of the '86ers' administration over to the Lions' operation. In fact, the '86ers were run out of the Lions' offices for a couple of years. When he sold the club to Stadnyk for *his* short-lived stay, it's said that he wound up showing a profit for his venture into our game—but I can almost guarantee it wouldn't have been much.

I had a lot of respect for Braley. Like Greg Kerfoot today, he paid his bills, stayed in the background on game day and never mentioned how much he had invested. At our first meeting he explained to me that he didn't know much about soccer. After a few games he'd say things like "Bob, shouldn't our defenders be *bigger*?" but he left the team to me and the coaching staff. You can't ask for better than that.

11

CANADIAN, EH?

"When they hold out the team jersey, it doesn't matter where you are or what you're doing. Everything else finishes second."

—Alex Bunbury, 1997

Picture this: Canada's national soccer team, standing in the infield of Edmonton's Commonwealth Stadium, staring up at the big scoreboard TV screen and watching Donovan Bailey, live from Toronto, run 150 metres to earn $1.5 million.

If you believed in irony, there was no shortage.

We were battling to stay alive in the qualifying round for the 1998 World Cup tournament in Paris. We had just beaten Costa Rica 1–0 on a goal by Eddie Berdusco, who hadn't played for Canada since 1994 and was there now only because injuries made our dressing room look like a *M*A*S*H* unit.

To get to the match our players had flown in from all over North America, Portugal and England. Tourist class, of course, and some of them on wildly zigzag routes to get on Air Canada flights because that way the CSA could bring them in on air miles points. Outside the stadium sat a charter bus—the players' luggage stowed aboard so they could save a night's hotel costs—that would take them back to the airport so they could fly back that night or early the next morning.

Call it a hunch, but I'd bet that when Bailey and Michael Johnson flew to Toronto for their match race they did not sit in economy or ride a bus to the hotel.

Team Canada's victory was worth $1,750 for each player, plus $250 for the one goal scored. For an essentially meaningless exhibition over a rarely run distance, Bailey and Johnson knew going in that the *least* they could earn was $500,000, and that the winner would get another $1 million.

At the packed Toronto press conference following the race, Bailey called Johnson "chicken" for pulling up lame after 110 metres and suggested that he wasn't hurt at all, merely faking the injury because he was being badly beaten.

In Edmonton, our guys told a handful of reporters that Costa Rica was a fine team and admitted we weren't a bunch of world-class players, just a good side that had to play as a team to have a chance, and how proud they were to play for Canada.

We stood in that infield and cheered Bailey's victory because he was Canadian, an Olympic sprint champion and the world's fastest man. Across the country, several million people were no doubt saying the same thing. Our own victory in our struggle to represent our country in the world's biggest sporting spectacle would be greeted, we knew, with national indifference.

No one was complaining. No one begrudged Bailey and Johnson the money. So it was a show biz shot, all manufactured glamour and outrageous hype. They were professional athletes. The opportunity came, and they took it. Good on 'em.

Still, as I looked around that infield, I felt a surge of pride at the dedication and commitment our guys continued to show as they donned that Canada jersey. And I wondered if the day would ever come when Canadians in numbers would truly understand.

Unless they've fallen victim to an outbreak of Phil Woosnam disease, which we'd thankfully believed to have been eradicated by the death of the NASL, no one in Canadian soccer is silly enough to believe that our game will ever come close to replacing hockey in the minds and hearts of Canadian sports fans. In our country, soccer is a niche market and is covered accordingly, although the arrival of the MLS has sparked new and promising media interest. Nonetheless, it got frustrating, sometimes, to see how much our players were putting into the World Cup drive and how little recognition they were getting in return.

In 1993 we were opening the second round of World Cup qualification in Tegucigalpa against Honduras. The game was available on satellite. In fact, TSN was picking it up—but not to carry live. Oh, no. Not when kickoff clashed with the Valvoline 200 from Phoenix, an auto race that American TV was taping to run on a delayed basis. Not when the auto race was followed by the Monster Truck Challenge, in which trucks so huge they'd look right at home in the Transformers sci-fi movies climb over piles of junk metal that used to be cars. Not when, after the car race and the truck challenge, Sports Centre was going to regurgitate scores from around the world. Not when that would be followed by a regular-season game featuring the Toronto Maple Leafs, who were already in the playoffs, and the Philadelphia Flyers, who couldn't get into them unless a handful of teams declared bankruptcy.

Canada's World Cup drive could wait until 9:30 p.m. PST, only seven-and-a-half hours after the game, which meant that, providing soccer fans had shut off the radio and TV, spoken to no one and taken the phone off the hook, they could watch their national team play a match that really mattered.

I'm not shooting at TSN—television networks look at ratings and demographics—but the NHL season that year was 1,066 games long, followed by playoffs that, should every series go the full seven games, could last 105 more. In the year 1066, as Jim Taylor has pointed out repeatedly in columns mocking the extended playoffs, William the Conqueror played the Saxons sudden-death, and won England. No playoffs, just one showdown. This one time, didn't a national soccer team out-rank the Leafs? Apparently not.

In the NHL, no one gets penalized for missing the world championship tournament. A player says he's tired or has an owie or family commitments, and that's that. The coach might be pissed off, Hockey Canada might be in a snit, but the final decision is his. In soccer, FIFA has an inflexible rule: club teams *must* free up their players for international competitions, and pay their regular club salary while they're gone. Once a player makes the commitment to the national team, he is there for keeps or until he's cut. If he grows disenchanted or wants time off to go back to his club for, say, a cup competition, the national coach can prohibit it.

Players who are asked to join the national team *can* refuse the honour. In countries where the game is everything it would be highly unlikely. To refuse would be a disgrace. In Canada, where the sport is still struggling for national recognition, it would be easier to say no—and in some cases tempting—because there's a catch to the FIFA rule that puts them under enormous pressure: club teams have to free them up and continue to pay them in their absence, but there's no rule saying they have to *play* them when they come back. Many a Team Canada player in my coaching years heard a manager say, "I can't stop you from going, but I have to fill your spot when you're *gone*, and the man who's there while you're gone just might stay there when you get *back*."

Craig Forrest was bitten twice.

A groin injury suffered while playing for Canada cost him much of the '92–'93 season. When he was ready to return, Ipswich Town was not ready to play him, not when he'd be leaving again to join Team Canada for round two. Now Ipswich was in training for their new season, which would open the night before he was supposed to be in Canada's nets for a game in Sydney, Australia. A plea to the CSA to let him skip that one game and go back to Ipswich to try to protect his job or win it back was rejected on the grounds that if one exception was made, requests by others would follow.

Could it hurt his career? Yes. Five weeks earlier he'd signed a two-and-a-half-year contract, and he'd yet to be with the club that had given it to him. When you're a youngster on the way up, as

Craig was then, exposure is everything. You have to be seen performing at top level so scouts for other teams can see you and hopefully report that you'd be worth buying.

At the other end of the spectrum, veterans like Frank Yallop and Colin Miller, not signed to the big contracts and nearing the end of their careers, ran the risk in staying with us of not being offered *any* contract. In the middle, youngsters like Mark Watson and Lyndon Hooper, who had contracts with English clubs, could only suffer from missed training.

There was always a certain amount of bitching. In the second round of the World Cup qualification in 1993, as I sat in an Edmonton hotel on the eve of the first half of our last-gasp home-and-home series against Australia, there was even some doubt that Team Canada would show up.

The players had decided they wanted bigger match fees, which wasn't going to happen because those things are set by FIFA, whose motto on anything remotely resembling change should be "Budge? Never!" The players were militant. No increase, no play. CSA president Kevin Pipe had just called.

"Bobby," he said, "there might not be a game."

"Okay," I said. "Just let me know."

I couldn't believe it would go that far. Money was money, but in the end national pride would kick in—which, in the wee hours, it did. Nonetheless, as a former player, I could empathize with them, not so much over the money as over some of the ludicrous situations they had to endure when they were the ones making sacrifices to be there.

Players on the squad during the Krautzun coaching days still shake their heads at the memories of a 1975 bus trip in Cuba en route to a friendly match in Havana. They bounced over a winding, dusty road for what seemed like forever. It was hot and dry, and the bus had no air conditioning. The sun beat in through the windows on one side, scorching those unlucky enough to be seated there, while the other side was comparatively shady.

Krautzun assessed the situation and made his decision.

"All first team players take seats on the shady side," he instructed. "Subs on the sunny side."

The players couldn't believe it, but made the switch. What Eckhard hadn't considered was that the road was really windy. Pretty soon, the sun was beating in on the other side. He was equal to the challenge.

"Change back," he said.

You couldn't fault him on consistency. Throughout his stay with the Whitecaps and with the national side he thought only of the guys who'd be playing that game. Subs were people to be ignored unless they became starters and were cast aside until it happened. Two years after the Cuba bus caper, the Whitecaps were in the dressing room at Queens Park, New Westminster, preparing for an exhibition game against Rochester. The room was small and overcrowded. Again, Eckhard had the answer.

"Everybody who's not starting, *get out*," he yelled. "You're stealing the oxygen of those who'll be playing!"

Stay on the national team long enough and you're bound to experience things that the CSA would not like to see gracing their Team Canada inducement program. For example, take the 1991 Honduran elevator incident.

In those days the early World Cup qualifiers were not home-and-home affairs; they just gathered the teams in one spot and played a round robin. So there we were in Tegucigalpa for five weeks, and in our hotel there was one constant: when a bunch of players got in an elevator, it jammed. This time, the doors were stuck apart by about four inches and we could see about a foot of the floor above. Those of us in the elevator were not a happy group, particularly me, being slightly claustrophobic.

There are armed guards at the elevators, and they are not the "Yeah-I've-got-a-gun-but-I'd-never-use-it" types we're used to here. These guys had some kind of submachine-guns and looked like they were itching for the chance to see if they worked. We're yelling at them to get somebody, push a button, do *something*, but they speak no English.

Then one of them gets an idea. He sticks the barrel of his gun through the crack in the door and starts prying it back and forth, trying to force the doors to open. All we can see is the gaping muzzle, which looks about a foot across.

We're team members, right? We think alike, and all we can think of is "What if his finger is on the trigger? What if he slips? What if the prying sets it off?"

You've never seen such teamwork. As one man, we hit the floor.

Every player who's travelled with the national team has stories like that: hotel rooms rifled, stomachs rebelling at unfamiliar food, endless hours waiting for planes or buses that seldom get there on time. But we call them, and they come. I suspect they always will.

In 1997, less than twenty-four hours after a 4–0 Sunday loss in Mexico City, some of them were on planes to Europe for mid-week games with the clubs that provided their livelihood. They played on consecutive Wednesdays, then climbed back on a plane on the Thursday morning to fly to Palo Alto for our game against Team USA. We lost 3–0. The next morning they boarded another plane to return to Europe.

As they were leaving, a Canadian reporter asked them why they would do that, particularly since Canada's chance of getting to the World Cup finals seemed well beyond wishful thinking. They looked at him as though he were crazy. They were playing for their country. What kind of an idiotic question was that?

12

MONTEZUMA'S REVENGE

"If Team Canada owned Hell and Estadio Azteca,
they'd live in Hell and rent Azteca out."
—*Calgary Sun*, March 3, 1997

I took over the national team in 1992 on my second try for the job. Tony Waiters had left the position after our great run to the '86 World Cup and was replaced by Bob Bearpark, who was replaced in turn in 1988 by former under-20's coach Tony Taylor. He was therefore in charge for the heartbreaking, close-but-no-cigar attempt to get past the first round qualification for the 1990 World Cup, which stands as a monument to the silliness of FIFA's away-goals rule. To advance to the next round in 1988 we had to get past Guatemala in a home-and-home series. We lost 1–0 on their home turf, came back home and beat them 3–2, which by any logic but FIFA's should have meant a third game or even a showdown at the penalty spot.

But, no. Under FIFA rules (and, to be fair, the rule was common knowledge), in the event of a two-game split the series would go to the team with the most goals on the other team's home ground because, gosh, it's much harder to score when you're not playing at home. Guatemala had two goals in defeat in our park, we had none in theirs. Goodbye, Canada. I remember driving home after the second game, listening to the local sportscast. "Canada beat Guatemala 3–2 today, but lost on the away-goals rule," the guy said. "Don't ask me what that means, because I have no idea."

Tony Taylor took the bullet for that one and the national team was all but shut down for a year, with only two friendlies in the entire season, against Denmark and Belgium, both 2–0 losses, with one B. Lenarduzzi as a sort of interim coach. I applied for the full-time job but by that time Waiters had decided to take another shot at it. He took the Olympic team on an unsuccessful qualifying run, decided he'd had enough, and the job came open again. I re-applied, this time I got it—and back to school I went.

First lesson: these weren't the '86ers, where my objective was to entertain, win or lose, so we could sell more season tickets and get the casual fans back for another look. This was World Cup qualifying, where it didn't matter how you won or drew as long as you did. On a team without a lot of scoring potential, that meant defend first and try to cash in your own chances when they came.(Just call me Eckhard.)

The first round, lumped in with Jamaica, Bermuda and El Salvador, went fine. We finished second with two wins, three draws and one loss to El Salvador, whom we joined three months later in the next round, along with Honduras and Mexico. That's when the fun started.

We opened in Honduras, where referee Noel Smith finished the match no better than even money to get out of the stadium alive. He started by awarding us a penalty—which John Catliff converted to give us an early lead—on a call so dubious that it earned him and his linesmen a selection of hurled bottles that, at five cents apiece, could have bought him the new set of glasses he clearly needed.

We were up 2–1 in injury time, holding on for dear life, when Smith ruled that Mark Watson had played the ball with his hand and called the penalty, which Honduras converted for the 2–2 draw. Watching the replay later, it seemed clear that the ball had hit

Watson on the hip, bounced up and came off the inside of his lower arm, clearly unintentionally. In no way did it hit his hand. Besides, the play should have been stopped before the call was made, when Randy Samuel was chopped down as he defended that final onslaught.

Our guys surrounded Smith, protesting the call. The Hondurans were there, too, protesting the *first* penalty call against them. Smith looked nobly sincere as he insisted that both calls had been accurate and fair—the same look, one Canadian media report recalled, that Ben Johnson had worn the day he insisted he'd never used steroids.

Neither side was buying it. Smith left the field inside a ring of soldiers, looking like the governor had called just as the executioner was about to pull the hood over his head. As for us, we were upset by the loss but cheered by the consolation prize. A point on the road was a point on the road, and Honduras had been favoured to go through to the next round.

Certainly the Honduran fans thought so. Totally unimpressed by such a narrow victory, they surrounded the Team Canada bus as it inched out of its spot in the stadium concourse, jeering and shaking their fists. At first we thought it was kind of funny and rolled down the windows to exchange what we thought would be the usual post-game insults. Then the crowd got bigger, the screaming got louder, and they started rocking the bus.

We rolled up the windows as the rocking got worse, waiting for the police to jump in. We never saw a single cop. Who knows, maybe they were too busy helping the locals with the bus-rocking, but it got kind of scary before we finally made it out onto the road.

When we came home for a two-game stand, beat El Salvador 2–0 and followed that with a 3–1 win over Honduras, things were looking pretty rosy, particularly after the El Salvador game, because in that one a gamble I'd taken in setting the roster for this second round had paid off.

On international experience alone, Mike Sweeney had to be on the squad. Only Bruce Wilson had more Canadian caps than Sweeney. Mike had been with us in '86, but he was nearing his thirty-second birthday and had played exactly three competitive games in two years—against Mexico in Victoria in 1990 and two friendlies against the US in '92. He was retired, married with two kids, studying law in Cleveland and coaching a bunch of junior college kids in his spare time.

I took a little media heat in naming him with a bunch of young guys trying to make our team. I was a rookie head coach, they said, supposed to be rebuilding the national team, not resurrecting it. But I kept remembering how accurate Mike had been with crosses on set pieces. Now, against El Salvador, we were looking at defenders who averaged 5'7", marking John Catliff at 6'3" and Alex Bunbury at 6'1". If we had a guy who could arch the ball in with pace and accuracy . . .

Mike's conditioning was open to question, although he'd been running and playing with his college kids, pushing them and himself until they thought the workouts would never end. I crossed my fingers, ignored the legs, and bet on the head—and it paid off. Sweeney lofted two marvellous crosses from the left corner, and Catliff and Bunbury climbed invisible ladders to nod them into the net with defenders about waist high.

It was a glorious way to begin the home stand, but one thing puzzled me: How could 2,000 El Salvadorians make so much more noise than the 4,800 Canadians jammed into Swangard Stadium that it sounded like we were playing a road game? This was our country, our city, our park, and when we took the traditional pre-match walk around the field, the horns and the whistles and the non-stop singing and cheering by the local El Salvadorian community made us feel like tourists whose next stop would be the airport for the flight home.

Still, things seemed to be going our way. Another hunch had paid off in the Honduras game, a move I'd made with regret. Dale Mitchell, so much the heart and soul of our team, had struggled through the first half. We were down 1–0. Word had already come that Mexico had beaten El Salvador, which pushed them one point ahead of us unless we could come back and get the win. And in this round, the top team advanced and everybody else went home. So

I mentally crossed fingers and subbed young Dominic Mobilio—nine international appearances, no goals—for Mitchell.

Dominic made me look like a genius, taking a pass from Bunbury that found him just outside the six-yard box and about three yards from the touch line. He coolly left-footed across the box at what looked like an impossible angle, and damned if it didn't curve into the top corner. The half wasn't five minutes old, and he'd tied it at 1–1. Ten minutes later Sweeney curled a ball into the jammed goalmouth area and somehow into the net off the goalie, although Catliff was credited with it. John then put one in from the spot after a questionable penalty call. We won 3–1 to go back to the top of the pack and off to Mexico where, naturally, everything came unravelled.

It's not just playing in Estadio Azteca that can drive visiting teams crazy in Mexico. Sometimes, it's the Mexicans.

Armed guards surrounded Azteca to keep foreigners from watching their team practice. The Mexican Football Association barred our team from the pitch after we'd ridden a bus for fifty minutes to get to a workout arranged for and promised earlier in the day. These were stringent precautions against a team already written off in a newspaper report informing the world that Mexico had played a practice game against a third division team earlier in the week "to become accustomed to playing an opponent of lesser technical skills."

But, in the end, they made it look like their assessment was correct. The 4–0 whipping we took that day was worse than embarrassing because, despite the altitude, the lack of oxygen, the roars and the occasional bag of urine, we had somehow held them scoreless through the first half.

People in the stands were upset. Heading into the match, despite the fact that we led the qualifying group, the local media had dismissed us. The front page story in the morning sports section of the Mexican *Daily News* the day we arrived was word that quarterback Joe Montana had jumped from the San Francisco 49ers to the

Kansas City Chiefs. We were second-page stuff because, as columnist Ricardo Castillo wrote:

"For all its importance in reaching the World Cup, Sunday's match between Mexico and Canada does not have the frills and thrills that matches against Honduras and El Salvador had. While the traditional sports enmity between Mexico and its Central American counterparts goes beyond reasonable limits, Mexico and Canada lack any rivalry to speak of."

But after forty-five minutes we were scoreless. Getting annihilated, yes. Lucky not to be down by two or three, yes. But scoreless. Walking off the field and listening to the home crowd booing their own team unmercifully, I thought, "If we can have that kind of luck for another forty-five minutes, we could sneak out of here with a draw."

We came out after the interval, and the players couldn't move their legs. Altitude, fatigue and the fifteen minutes sitting in the dressing room stiffening up made them feel like they wore anvils instead of soccer boots. It was downright humiliating. We hadn't played well all day, and allowing them to score two quick ones late in the game could wind up screwing us on goal differential if we wound up tied with someone for second place.

Not that we were out of it. The 2–1 win in San Salvador kept us one point behind Mexico, and we'd meet them in our final game of the round a week later in Toronto. Win there, and we'd go to the World Cup. Finish second and we'd be forced into a back-door ordeal for the one remaining spot, a home-and-home series with Australia. But we weren't even considering that. Mexico on the road was not the unbeatable team from Estadio Azteca. The edge was still Mexico's. We had to win; for them, a draw would do. But at home, we'd have a shot.

The CSA got hammered for what happened next, but there was a certain logic to it when the decision was made. Heading into the second round, when we hadn't looked all that good going into the first, it sold the rights to the final game in Toronto to Karsten Von Wersebe, owner of the Toronto Blizzard, taking cinch cash early rather than risk losing money on a game that could well be meaningless should we be out of the running before it was played. Now he was looking smart and the CSA was looking silly, because Mexico was coming in with a World Cup spot on the line and he could make a pot full of money that could have been the association's.

All I knew was that we were playing at home and that with a packed Varsity Stadium cheering for us the emotion could carry us to victory. In three short hours we could be planning a trip to the World Cup!

We went out for the walk-around, looked into the stands—and saw a sea of green. It was the El Salvador-at-Swangard Stadium story all over again. Three-quarters of the crowd were Mexican! The drums were banging, the singing was loud and endless. It was like Estadio Azteca without the urine bags.

Our guys were looking at each other in wonderment. What the hell *was* this? But they shook it off, played a pretty good half and went up 1–0 on a goal by Bunbury. If we could just hold on . . .

We couldn't. Hugo Sanchez tied it just before the half, and now the pressure was on us, because a draw was good enough for Mexico to go through.

It wasn't to be. We thought we had the lead when Lyndon Hooper put the ball in the net off a cross by Peschisolido, only to have the linesman rule the play offside. On the replay it looked iffy, but it still left us needing to push everybody up trying for the win. We got caught, they scored, and we were down and done, 2–1.

Not dead, though. Zombies, maybe, but still kicking. Win the back-door, home-and-home series with Australia and we could still sneak into the big show. As it turned out, it was as though Somebody Up There had decided it really wasn't to be.

Consider:

We go to Edmonton to get ready for the first game. We've already lost Catliff, who landed wrong during a workout and blew a knee. Now we're playing a harmless little five-on-five game, plastic cones for goalposts, no bodily contact, and David Norman winds up on the ground with extended ligaments. He's gone, and so is Grant Needham, the Montreal Impact striker rushed in to replace Catliff. He was in his hotel room and got an eye infection. How does that happen?

"Hotel movies?" a media guy suggested. "Some of those things should come with free penicillin. I remember one where there's this cheerleader, and she . . ."

"Thank you for that," I said.

We were reeling, but a crowd of just under 30,000 cheered us on and we won 2–1 on a goal by Mobilio. Forrest was hot and kept us in after a shot went off Nick Dasovic for an own-goal. Shows you how smart I was. I'd gone public days earlier, saying I couldn't understand why an important game like this would be put in *Edmonton* when we could have gone back to Toronto where, now that Mexico was safely in the World Cup, the crowd could relax and get behind us. Had to eat a lot of crow for that.

So, off we went to Sydney, a win up, the team brimming with confidence. My own emotions weren't nearly as upbeat. My dad's condition was worsening. I knew he could pass while I was away. I thought of staying home, but a talk with family and friends convinced me otherwise. "He wouldn't want to be the reason you didn't go with the team," they said. "You know what he'd say if you asked him: 'Go, it's a big opportunity.'"

I knew they were right. A strong man, my dad. He knew the family was struggling with the thought of losing him. "Don't feel bad," he told me. "I'm eighty-two, and if someone had told me at twenty that I'd make it this far I'd have thought 'Great!' I've had four good boys and a wonderful home and life. I'd prefer to live on, but no regrets." He was dying, but worrying about us.

The Aussies came out, and for fifteen minutes they simply destroyed us and went up 1–0. But for Forrest, who was absolutely unbelievable, it would have been over, and he had the Aussie coach Eddie

Thomson shaking his head as we walked off the field. "We're kickin' 'em in," he marvelled, "and you're kickin' 'em out."

Halfway though the second half, Hooper lets one go and, just like that, we've tied the match, we lead the series 3–2 on aggregate and all we have to do is hold on. Then Forrest and Randy Samuel have a communication gap, each thinking the other is going for a ball in the box. An Aussie knifes in, pops the ball over Craig's head, and we're going into overtime. I felt bad for us and especially Craig, who'd saved our bacon again and again.

But we'd had our chance, and you know what happens when you blow one of those. Overtime settled nothing, we lost 4–1 on penalty kicks, and the World Cup dream was over. It would be weeks before the numbness went away, and four years before we could make another try.

13

LOST IN TRANSLATION

"How could such a thing happen? Who could do *such a thing?"*
> —Police escort officer, San Salvador, 1997

T he gorgeous translation lady fielded the question raised in Spanish by an El Salvador TV guy, put some English on it, and headed it over to me. "Is it your intention to esplode your players?" she asked earnestly.

It being my first season as Team Canada coach—and she *was* gorgeous—I pointed out that, since we'd lost only one match to date in the second round of '94 World Cup qualifying, exploding my players would be a tad premature even though that loss had been a 4–0 pasting in Mexico the day before. "Maybe if we lose here on Sunday," I joked. "But not before."

She relayed the answer. The TV guy looked puzzled and cut loose with another torrent of Spanish. She listened carefully, then gave me a dazzling smile.

"Esploit!" she said triumphantly. "He means *esploit*. How do you plan to get your players to *esploit* the El Salvador players?"

By now I had it figured that joking wasn't going to get it done.

Not when another TV guy who spoke English was demanding an interview with goalie Craig Forrest to have him 'splain how he let in four goals against Mexico. "My youngest child could have prevented that first goal!" he exploded.

The temptation was to ask him to trot out his youngest child for a shootout against Forrest, even though it would be unfair to Craig because the El Salvador guy had scouted us and we had no game tape on the way his kid played.

But I was learning: in Central America, you do not joke about soccer. It is far too important. And the guy wasn't being snotty. We'd just been handed our asses by the Mexicans. To have no one punished, to sit there as I was doing, saying we would put it behind us and try to learn from the experience, was *unthinkable*. How could a game mean so *little*?

It's something I doubt the non-soccer North American sports fan will truly understand, perhaps because our lifestyles are so different. In Canada hockey is everything, but fans don't commit suicide when the home team loses. Seldom does a World Cup competition go through to the hoisting of the Jules Rimet Trophy without one or more reports of a tearful fan taking his own life or, at the very least, hurling his TV-viewing chair out the window.

For Canadians, hockey is a vital thread in our cultural fabric, but it's not the whole damned suit. Kids who want to play the game sign up, put on expensive, professional-style equipment and get driven to winter clubs or skating rinks where the ice is carefully tended, the dressing rooms are warm and leak proof, and post-game trips to a McDonald's are part of the ritual. How can they identify with the barefoot village kids in Central America, racing over a playground playing *their* national game, booting a ball that, in the poorer areas, they've made themselves out of rags and old clothes stuffed together and kicked until it falls apart?

Hockey is part of our life, but to the soccer nations their game is the reason man was put on the planet—which is why, the morning after the drubbing in Mexico, the media there were demanding my view on the Salvadoran Football Association president's statement that his country's national team would lie down against Canada in order to make things more difficult for Mexico in the standings.

I laughed. Clearly, the idea was ridiculous, probably the product of some Mexican version of the *National Enquirer*, right next to word that Hitler had been seen working in a Brazilian gas station.

"No, no," the media types insisted. The statement had, indeed, been made, and how did I feel about it?

"I'd like to shake the President's hand," I grinned, and shrugged it off, but by the time we got to San Salvador the story had taken on new life. Now it wasn't the president of the Salvadoran Football Association who was supposed to have said it. Now it was the president of the whole damned country.

The El Salvador media did not take it well, and sprang to their nation's defence. Such a statement was never made. El Salvador's team would never deliberately yield to an opponent. Pride aside, it would be *unethical*.

In Canada, where the game is merely a sport, the story would never have run unconfirmed. In the soccer-mad nations of Central America, where *futebol* is everything, even the ridiculous reports/ rumours must be given serious headline consideration. So, what did I think about it? And no more jokes, please—this is serious business. It got even more serious when we won the match 2–1 on goals by Catliff and Mobilio. Who cared now what the president had or hadn't said. El Salvador was in grave danger of *failing to advance*, and that would be a national disaster.

We got out of town—a lot more easily, as it turned out, than on our next visit.

Even knowing the national mania from previous experience, road trips into Central America can bring visiting teams up short. Consider Team Canada's qualifying swing in 1997 . . .

In Mexico's Estadio Azteca, soft drinks are served in sealed plastic pouches to eliminate temptation among the 130,000 or so fans who might otherwise be inclined to rain bottles or cans down on the visiting team's bench. We soon learned that the fans were equal to the challenge. They opened the bags, drank the liquid, peed into the bags, sealed them again and let fly.

In most stadiums that wouldn't have been a problem, but in Estadio Azteca the sightline seating angle is so severe that people seem to be clinging for support and the field is so tight to the stands that the benches are well within hurling distance. That explains how a bag of urine managed to land in the lap of my assistant coach, Alan Errington.

Alan was equal to the occasion. He poked at the bag with a finger, held the finger to his nose, and said, "Female! And three months pregnant!"

You know the fuss around NHL arenas at Stanley Cup time, where security people wander the stands looking for fans who've smuggled in octopi to throw onto the ice? Well, on game day in Kingston, Jamaica, the mayor runs a plea on the front page of the morning paper urging the 30,000-plus fans who'll jam National Stadium to remember the rules: no firearms, knives, bottles, stones or other weapons allowed, but if you feel the need to bring your gun, kindly leave it at the stadium door with the police for safekeeping and pick it up when you leave.

In San Salvador, the craziness began at the match meeting twenty-four hours before kickoff, when a Salvadoran Football Association official began by assuring us that "there will be no trouble" at the match.

"But if you *win*," he cautioned, "do not attempt to return to your dressing room. Go to the centre of the pitch and we will take you out by helicopter."

Yes, he admitted, there had been some problems when Mexico won here 1–0. "Some problems," we found out later, translated into a riot involving several thousand fans. When the Americans took the field for a match that ended 1–1, the crowd in the section called Vietnam ("No sane person goes there," said a waiter at the hotel) unfurled a long banner reading AMERICANS! WELCOME TO VIETNAM!

But for our match, no problems! Precautions had been taken, we were assured, and sure enough, come game time the pitch was ringed by police, armed and in full body armour, helmets with facial visors and knee-to-shoulder crowd-control shields. To complete the homey touch, two helicopters circled overhead, each with a machine-gun-bearing soldier dangling from a ladder.

Word of the move to centre field if we won did not sit well with our media, who noted that the bench that served as a press box was simply a regular row of the stadium stands, smack in the middle of the home crowd. "If you win," they asked, "how do *we* get out?"

We checked, and the answer was a shrug. Incidentally, it's easy to spot members of the unbiased Central American soccer media. They're usually wearing team jerseys and they cheer when their team scores. For game-winning goals, they have been known to sing and dance around the press area.

Don't misunderstand. When they travel to North America, they probably think our media are strange for *not* cheering and dancing.

Say what you like about unruly fans, no one can question their commitment. The stadium gates opened at 6:30 a.m., five hours before kickoff. By 7:45, in a city where ticket prices ran from $8 down to $6 US and the minimum wage was $6 US per week, all but a few of the 38,000 seats were filled.

I regret to say that we took great care of our Canadian media, losing 4–1. The violence was purely vocal—the continual cries of "Cinqo! Cinqo!" as the crowd demanded a fifth goal and the throat-slitting motions of the exiting mob as they lined up to jeer good-naturedly at the Canadian bus.

But San Salvador wasn't through with us yet.

The next morning we gathered at 5 a.m. in the hotel lobby to board the police-escorted team bus to the airport, and most of the players' equipment bags were loaded into a small van, along with the large and thankfully locked cases containing medical supplies, soccer balls and such. Had we not all been half-asleep we might have noticed that the van driver seemed in a great rush to get loaded and gone. "Hurry! Hurry!" he insisted, tugging at our bags. Then he jumped into the van and drove off, about five, maybe ten minutes before we boarded the bus.

We got to the airport and looked around. No van. It didn't arrive for another ten minutes, and once again the driver was in an all-fired hurry to get the players to grab their bags and scram.

Forrest picked his up and frowned.

"Seems a little light," he said.

I opened my own bag. Four team jerseys, each signed by all the players and earmarked for charity auctions, were missing. Now the hunt was really on as players checked their own bags over the protests of officials who insisted we might miss our plane. The losses began to mount: team jerseys, sweat pants, soccer boots.

We informed our police escort. They were stunned. How could such a thing happen? Who could do such a thing?

Well, let's examine the clues.

The luggage is packed in a van for a non-stop trip to the airport. It leaves five or ten minutes before the bus, but arrives ten minutes *after*. It has a driver and an aide. No one else was aboard. Gosh, Inspector Clousseau, could these men possibly be *suspects*? Or maybe it was banditos, stopping the van at gunpoint in a desperate bid to obtain a coveted Paul Peschisolido jersey.

The police talk to the van crew, with much gesturing. No, they say, the van never stopped. So how did the gear disappear from closed suitcases in a moving van? Truly, a great mystery, señor. That such a thing should happen!

Coffee is sipped while the police ponder. The players are growing more upset by the moment. The plane, we're warned, is about to leave. On the sidewalk, spectators are smiling a lot. They do not seem surprised at the crime. Don't worry, the police assure us, this will be investigated!

For a man presumably facing further interrogation, the van driver seems remarkably calm, perhaps because the policeman with him is sharing a laugh and a cigarette.

I shoo the players aboard the plane, mulling over the final irony: The airport tax to get into El Salvador was $10 US. The fee to leave is $25 US. Flying home, we all agree that it is cheap at the price. Maybe we *should have* exploded their players.

That '97 swing was also when we discovered, to our horror, that sex had done us in. Not the kind that Krautzun worried about during his stint as head coach of the old Whitecaps, the kind that sapped players' strength, sabotaged their concentration and, or so legend had it, might cause blindness or at least the need for glasses. No. This was retroactive sexual activity in other countries.

We ran into it the day we arrived in Palo Alto, CA, for our game against the Americans. At the press conference, US officials introduced us to two new players you might call instant Yankees, German-born and raised and currently playing in the Bundesliga, but sired by Americans stationed in that country a couple of decades earlier and therefore eligible to play for the US team because of dual citizenship. They both sounded like there'd been a casting call for *Hogan's Heroes*.

Forward David Wagner was a teammate of midfielder Thomas Dooley, who was also raised in Germany but got his dual citizenship way back in, let's see, 1992. Dooley found out that Wagner had an American father and recruited him just in time to get him on the US roster for the second round of qualifying. The game against us would be his second as an American.

And then there was midfielder Michael Mason, a.k.a Dotcom, so nicknamed because US coach Steve Sampson had heard of him via an e-mail tip from the American fan club, Sam's Army. Mason's father, stationed in Germany, married there and raised seven children, all of whom spoke English except for Michael, who told us through an interpreter that "I feel like an American. It is an honour to play for the United States."

We lost 3–0, in great part due to the speed of one Ernie Stewart, a dual-citizenship guy raised in the Netherlands by a Dutch mother, who flashed past our defenders like they'd taken root.

The US talent hunt did not end there. When they qualified and went to Paris, their roster included David Regis, a Frenchman born in Martinique who was a defender for Karlsruhe in the Bundesliga and who'd become an American only a month earlier by virtue of his US wife, Nikki. He'd quickly learned to sing "The Star Spangled Banner," though with a thick Gallic accent, but that was about the limit of his English. Teammates communicated with him through sign language.

You have to hand it to the US Soccer Association. Normally there was a mandatory three-year wait after marrying a US citizen before the spouse could apply for citizenship, but the process could be sped up if the US spouse worked abroad. So the federation helped Nikki find a job in France—with the travel firm that had a business deal with US Soccer.

Six months after the Palo Alto thumping, sex reared its ugly head again. The Jamaican side we'd played to a scoreless draw in April, desperate for scorers, had scoured the British soccer registry and come up with four players who were born in Jamaica but whose families had moved to other lands shortly after the first diaper change. Three were on the roster of first division Portsmouth: a dazzling twenty-year-old striker named Deon Burton, who scored the goal that beat us 1–0; midfielder Fitzroy Simpson, who played a huge role; and striker Paul Hall, who had already scored six goals in eight games for his new and instant homeland. Midfielder Robbie Earl, captain of Wimbledon's Premier League side, was also suddenly one of the Reggae Boyz.

Not everyone in Jamaica was happy with the talent transfusion. The rest of the team, it was said, were in a bit of a snit, which was understandable. Jamaica had so very few players abroad, so the national side had been together for the better part of two years, slogging through the early qualifying rounds and dreaming the World Cup dream. Now four of them discovered they'd been replaced by guys whose knowledge of their native land was limited to, as one columnist suggested, "cram viewings of the John Candy movie about the Jamaican bobsled team." Jamaica's fans, on the other hand, thought it was great.

Were we upset at this influx of instant Americans and Jamaicans on teams we were trying to beat? Of course. Given the same opportunity, would we have used the same tactic for our *roster*? In a heartbeat. We just couldn't find anyone.

For Jim Taylor, writing in the *Calgary Sun*, it raised a vital question: what had *our* servicemen and overseas-stationed businessmen been doing while these other guys were out there in foreign lands giving their all?

> Where were *our* servicemen in Germany? Did they spend *all* their time at the front? Couldn't they have squeezed in enough R&R to fall in love with, or at least impregnate, enough of the local Frauleins to ensure a supply of potential dual-passported soccer stars that we could fast track on "O Canada" in time for World Cup qualifying?
>
> Have no Canadian salesmen found time in their world travels to leave their genetic and nationalistic imprint in countries where soccer isn't considered the feminine of slughim? Where were the traditional farmer's daughters of story, song and joke. Did our guys think they were only there to *sell*?
>
> Naturally, it is too late to go looking for unknown but potential instant Canadian stars in the leagues of the world, even if we wanted to, but if that's the way the game is to be played henceforth, Canadian peacekeepers and travelling salesmen are reminded that now is the time to begin preparing for World Cup 2018, and every man is expected to do his duty.
>
> So get out there, guys, and make one for the team. Just don't try to claim for the wine and the nylons.

Jim had posed a good question and, for Team Canada fans, an ideal solution—as long as the wives and girlfriends of our citizens overseas never found out.

14

DÉJÀ VU, DAMMIT!

*"Ask John Wayne, Randolph Scott, Hoot Gibson, Tom
Mix or any of the other cowboy greats who strode
into the other guy's town determined to save the day.
They'll all tell you the one great truth about going into
a gunfight: It's virtually imperative that you bring
bullets."*

—*Calgary Sun*, September 8, 1997

The frustrating thing about coaching, particularly at the national
level, is that once the players hit the pitch there's absolutely
nothing you can do except make up to three substitutions, shout
instructions, and hope.

And it's not just talent that makes the difference—sometimes,
it's player personalities. In some cases, the very competitive fire that
drove them to the professional level can do them in when the pressure is greatest. In others, their pride eventually blinds them to the
inevitable reality that they're just not good enough. And when the
media get involved . . .

Let me give you a couple of examples from our pursuit of a spot
in the 1998 World Cup.

We've come through the six-game first round with five wins and a draw, taken another 4–0 whipping at Estadio Azteca (aggregate score in our last three visits, 16–0) and been shut out 3–0 by the US in Palo Alto. But now we're home in Vancouver to face El Salvador, desperately needing to get on track. One reason for optimism: Paul Peschisolido.

Pesch was a fireball, a gifted, sometimes dazzling, little street fighter of a striker who seemed permanently cranky but, for the most part, ready to make the trip from England, where he'd built a career of wealth and success, to play for the country where he was named footballer of the year in 1996 (even if he didn't want to train once he got here). There was a chip on his shoulder, but for that kind of talent potential you make allowances, and he seemed to realize how much we were counting on him.

Unfortunately, at the 32-minute mark of a scoreless game against El Salvador, he came down with the stupids. As he and El Salvador's Wilfredo Iraheta battled for a ball in the corner, Pesch grabbed the top of the corner flag and snapped it into Iraheta's face.

Never mind that Iraheta reacted as though his nose was broken and allowed himself to be carried off on a stretcher before a recovery so rapid you'd think he'd made a quick trip to Lourdes. Pesch knew the rule on bringing the game into disrepute, knew the yellow card would be automatic and, since he'd already collected a yellow only minutes earlier, knew that the resulting red card would have him ejected from this game and suspended for our next game against Jamaica. Anyway, he snapped and he was gone, leaving us a man down and scrambling to settle for a scoreless draw in a game we needed to win.

Pesch is coaching now after a career in which he played for nine teams in England. I wonder, sometimes, how Pesch the coach would react if he had to deal with Pesch, the player.

Which brings us to the Domenic Mobilio story, so difficult to discuss now because Dom died suddenly in 2004 of an apparent heart attack at age thirty-five. So please understand, this is not about the young man whose talents would probably have kept him on the

179

team had he not been hit by injuries. This is about a coaching situation that turned into a public relations nightmare.

We'd played to another scoreless draw at home after the Pesch incident, this time against Jamaica, which gave us a tidy total of zero goals in four matches. Meanwhile, Domenic was on a scoring binge with the '86ers, with six goals in his last eight games. Some of the media added 2 plus 2 and got 5:

Why wasn't Mobilio back on the national team, and why hadn't Lenarduzzi picked him for this round in the first place?

Was I bypassing him for Sunday's game against Costa Rica because Domenic had publicly expressed his anger and disappointment at not being named to the side in the first place? Was there some personal reason why I wasn't making what, to the media at least, was a no-brainer decision?

That last one really annoyed me, because I did have my reasons for bypassing Dom, and they had nothing to do with anything but his abilities at the moment.

A severe hamstring pull had cost him much of the '95 season, and it seemed to me he was now a step slower. Yes, he had a hot streak going with the '86ers, but there was a world of difference between playing internationally and starring in a fledgling league manned by kids on their way up and vets on their way down. Dom was an opportunist and a potentially great one, but a lot of his success with us came through feeding off the strength and power of John Catliff, who owned the air, came down with elbows flying and created space in which Dom could collect the loose pieces. With Catliff gone, we were no longer tough in the middle, and much of that space was gone.

However, the big reason Dom hadn't made the squad had come in a fitness test in Florida as we prepared to open the round against Mexico. It was a twelve-minute session in which players were to run as far as they could, walk when they couldn't run any more, crawl when they couldn't walk, as long as they went for the full twelve minutes. Dom couldn't finish. His injuries had taken their toll on his speed as well as his stamina, and if he had no stamina in Florida, how long would he last in the altitude of Estadio Azteca?

He wanted it so badly. Telling him he hadn't made it wasn't easy. If his disappointment turned to anger that made him go public, that was in a way understandable because he was a competitor. What I *didn't* understand was the media preoccupation with getting him back on the squad, which went on for a couple of months.

Nonetheless, I kept quiet and didn't mention the Florida fitness run. Maybe, with time, he'd get back to his old playing level—everyone on the team was pulling for him—but when players were pressed by media types about whether they thought Dom should be on the squad, their silence should have been a telling response.

Besides, they had someone else on their minds during that Florida training session: striker Tomasz Radzinski, who spent most of his time sitting on the sidelines massaging his hamstring and saying no, he didn't really feel up to training today. Maybe tomorrow. The team doctors said he looked ready to them, but . . .

Tomasz was a talent we badly needed, a striker who later went on to score twenty-five goals in ninety-one games for Everton and eleven more in a three-year stint with Fulham. He'd proved his worth to the Canadian program when he came aboard in 1995, and would again in the early 2000s, but he clearly did not want to be with us. That ticked me off, because I had done him a huge favour by letting him skip one of our qualifying-round matches when it clashed with the Belgian Cup final he really wanted to play in back home.

I could have said "No," but instead I said, "Go, but you *owe* us." He agreed, but now there he was, sitting in Florida and obviously wishing he'd never come back.

There we were, riddled. Jason DeVos had gone home with a broken foot. So had Colin Miller, whose two yellow cards made him ineligible for the game in El Salvador anyway. We'd flown Jeff Clarke of the under-20 team in to replace Miller. Now we had to fly in Carl Fletcher to replace DeVos. And now we had a guy with a phantom hamstring pull?

It was probably just as well that Tomasz didn't make it to the practice field. Some of our players were ready to put the boots to him.

As to the overall qualifying round, it turned out to be eerily familiar to the one four years earlier: sail through the first round, get stomped in Estadio Azteca, and find goals as rare as hen's teeth. We scrapped, give our guys that. Burdusco's goal gave us the 1–0 win over Costa Rica in Edmonton and we dared to dream that maybe our shot at Paris was still there. We never ran out of try, we just ran out of goals. In our last four games we managed only three, two of them in a draw with Mexico in Edmonton. Not so tough away from Azteca, were they?

We were done, and this time there was no back-door reprieve.

I was done, too, and I was okay with that. In fact, I'd gone on record with the media saying that if we didn't qualify this time I was gone. Coaches have to win, no matter what the circumstances. I'd had two cracks at it and hadn't gotten it done. Fair enough.

I knew I'd grown as a coach. Looking back now, I realized my coaching career had gone through two phases. The first I brought with me from the '86ers—not a lot of tactical stuff, just "Hey, let's go play!" With them it had been fine because we usually had more firepower than the other guys and more often than not we'd win. It worked because the talent was there and the players had been around me for a few years and knew what was expected. With the national team, I came to realize the difference was massive.

I hadn't done a lot tactically in the first go-round. The players would fly in and I'd say, "How're you doing?" I'd put up the starting lineup and away we'd go. Although the ending had been a crushing disappointment, the run to qualifying for '94 had gone reasonably well, but for our second World Cup bid it was clear that the approach would have to change.

I'd never used video before. Now we were heavily into it, watching our own training and scouting the teams coming in. I had a great video guy, Dave Partridge out at University of BC, who'd spend hours breaking down the tape and editing it. It was a great help, but there was a trick to it, too: don't show the players too much at a time. They'll dial you out in five minutes. In today's digital world it's much easier, of course. There's no rolling tape back and forth—just push a button and you can call up any sequence you want—but go too long and they'd still nod off.

So much of the national team job is man management. You're not going to make better players out of guys who arrive two days before a match and leave the morning after. You're there to get the best out of them. One of the big jobs was with the subs, the guys who probably wouldn't be seeing any action in a specific game and knew it, keeping them motivated rather than pissed off, because ultimately you were going to need them and they had to stay ready for when the call came.

The other part of that is convincing players to do what they do best and forget about the rest. Sometimes that's not easy. Instead of using what they've got to the best of their ability, they look at what they'd *like* to be and mistakenly think they *can* be. Even the dependable ones can get the bug. Randy Samuel was in his mid-twenties during the '94 run, a big, strong guy who could run and tackle and shut people down. For a while he went through a phase where he wanted to be more involved in the offensive thrust, to bring the ball up from the back. To do that you have to be great with the ball, which he wasn't.

We recently had another example with the Whitecaps, a seventeen-year-old kid who'd been good enough to play in the league final against Montreal. The reason was that he was a pit bull and nobody liked playing against him, but people started bending his ear: got to be a better passer, got to dribble by people.

I tried to explain to him that he had a future in the game, but that people were going to pick him because of the things he did so well. If you're a good ball winner, win it and get it to someone who can play it. But he tried to change his game and kind of fell off the face of the earth. Sad.

I look back at the national team experience now and remember how proud I was of our guys, proud of the work ethic and the dedication, proud of the way Pesch had bounced back and run about 10,000 miles in perpetual effort as if to make up for the corner flag incident. Most of the memories will be cherished.

Not all, though. When the final qualifying round began in '97, I guess we were the victims of our down-to-the-last-game run in '93 and our 5–1–0 start in the first round this time around. Some of the very people who'd cheered us then just turned on us.

Coming out of Stanford after the 3–0 loss to the US, people were yelling, "You're done, Lenarduzzi," and screaming that I should be fired. I've never argued with their right to do that, but I remember thinking, "Wow! Two games, and they want my head." The knives were out, and they stayed out. When we played the US again, at Swangard Stadium (by which time we were out of the running), Denny Veitch took my son Ryan to the game and found people outside the gates handing out leaflets and yelling, "Sign this if you want Lenarduzzi fired!" I doubt whether it had any influence, but they got their wish.

When the CSA confirmed that a change would be made, I had no bad feelings. It's a results-oriented profession. I just didn't like the way people had taken the opportunity to pile on. However, I said nothing. Although I thought the whole system needed a shakeup that went far deeper than the coaching regime, I knew that anything I said would be considered sour grapes. It was time to move on.

15

AND NOW . . . WHAT??

"Those who cannot remember the past are condemned to repeat it."

—George Santayana, 1905

As I left the men's national program in November of 1997, the Canadian men's team stood sixty-third in the FIFA world rankings. Fourteen years and six head coaches later it stood, as of January 2011, at eighty-fourth.

The highest it ever got was fortieth, in December 1996 after our World Cup run. The lowest ever was in March 2007, when it sank to 107th. There's a message there somewhere, and I believe it is this: The system is broken—not beyond repair, but seriously wounded. Band-aids aren't the answer. What's required is major surgery, which should start by cutting off the head.

There are things the Canadian Soccer Association does superbly. This country's recreational soccer program is second to none, mostly because it is run by people who have been there in the trenches, handing out the oranges and making sure the nets are up and the fields are lined. However, letting the amateurs who've come up through that system into provincial executive bodies decide who should coach the national programs and how those programs should be run makes about as much sense as buckling the car seat behind the steering wheel and handing the baby the keys.

Why? Because their decisions will almost always be based on bias, on what's good for their province as opposed to what's good for the game in their country.

Look at where the men's program sits today. Our region, CONCACAF, now has three spots open for World Cup qualifying plus one back-door entry by facing the fifth-place South American team. Translation: Once you get past the first round, you have a better than 50 percent chance of qualifying. Say we concede two of those spots, based on their current status, to the US and Mexico. If we're doing our job properly, we should be finishing ahead of Honduras and Costa Rica (who are probably considered the toughest after the first two), but we haven't because we've never really addressed the root problem, which was and remains player development.

Why? Because the board of directors hasn't had the vision to think beyond the process that's crippled us for years: (a) elimination, (b) fire the coach and (c) let the new guy inherit the same problems that got the previous guy fired.

There is a move toward change, a vote taken to eliminate the provincial presidents from the board in a phasing-out progression that would be completed in 2015, at which point the board should be made up of business people and soccer people who don't have hidden agendas or provincial agendas and will make decisions based on what's good for the game.

Ideally, that should lead to a more sensible and logical approach to the technical side: look at what we're doing, establish a plan that looks at what we've done in the past, learn from it and accept the fact that it hasn't been very productive. The potential flaw is that between now and 2015 the provincial presidents have time to fight to keep their positions. Right now the board is polarized. There are those who put the game and the vision first, but do you think the rest of them are going to give up their right to wear those CSA jackets and make the trips to FIFA events without a fight? Not a hope.

Let's say there is a new and more knowledgeable board of directors with the clout, the know-how and the determination to put the national program on the right path. How do they do it? It's worth looking to the US Soccer Federation (USFA) and what it did in 1998 with what was called Project 2010.

As a first step, they brought in Portuguese coach Carlos Queiroz, twice an assistant to Sir Alex Ferguson at Manchester United. They gave him two years and told him to hit the road, tour the country, find out what was going on in the game and report back with a plan to fix it. Objective (gulp): win the World Cup by 2010.

I know people chuckled at that. But in 2002 they qualified and could easily have reached the semi-finals but for a missed hand ball call against Germany that could have tied it at 1–1 in the forty-ninth minute. Instead, Germany won 1–0. True, they haven't done as well recently, but they're at the point now where reaching the quarter-finals and losing has become unacceptable, whereas eight to twelve years ago it would have been viewed as a magnificent achievement.

Now, I know there's no way Canada can come anywhere near matching the $50 million the USFA reportedly pumped into Project 2010. But they *moved*, damnit! They brought a qualified person in to set up the plan, they put it together and they implemented it. We still haven't even acknowledged that we have a problem.

We need to get past that. Then it becomes a question of whether we want to go that route. Do we bring someone in from outside, do we establish a task force of people in this country who've been in the game at a high level or do we do a hybrid of the two? What? At least do *something* that will get the research done to establish what needs to be done until we get a professional infrastructure and a Canadian league for upcoming talent.

Once we've done that, we've got to make sure we've got the funding and the sponsors on board who want to take the ride with us, and don't kid yourselves—it's going to be a long ride, a marathon, not a sprint. The problem is, we don't have anyone in place right now who's prepared to look down the road, because instead of feeling they can be part of the process that triggers the eventual change, they worry first that they might not be there when it comes.

With that move to change the organizational structure by 2015, I actually think we might be on our way, although the first suggestion, to implement the change immediately, was shot down, so you could say that the old guard had a bit of a win in getting the three-year reprieve.

The trick will be to get the right people into place. Putting business people in charge of the whole thing would be pointless if, for all their business smarts, they know nothing about soccer. Turning the entire process over to soccer people wouldn't work if they lacked the background to deal with the business end. It will require a balance.

To start with, I'd suggest looking at the people running our three professional clubs. I've never asked or suggested it, but I'm sure that if Greg Kerfoot thought he had a chance to go in with a vision and an opportunity to put it into place, he would be interested in being part of the new structure. Then there are the people from Maple Leafs Sports and Entertainment, who run the Toronto franchise, and Joey Saputo of the Montreal Impact, who will be entering the MLS next season. They love the game, they've put up the money for their franchises and they're committed long term. Don't you think they might have some good ideas on how to move the national side to a higher level?

On the business side, we need people who may know little or nothing about the game but understand television and marketing, have the ability to go into the marketplace and make things happen, to go out and get the money, and then turn the process over to the soccer people and give them the opportunity to put their technical expertise into play.

As for picking the national coach, what experience do the

provincial presidents have? Maybe they coached their kids in rec soccer, maybe they just brought oranges—and good for them—but how does that qualify them for picking the guy to run the national team? It's flawed. Why not go to someone like Tony Waiters or me and ask for our input? We've *been* there. Isn't it possible we might have some thoughts on what's required? Go to another country and ask for recommendations. In the English FA, do you think it's the politicians and the badgers who are picking the coach?

The country's professional teams have four votes now that Edmonton has a franchise in Division II, which makes us insignificant unless the badgers wind up in a tie. Players and alumni? One vote for the women, one for the men. The rest of the votes—700-plus, last time I checked—are based on the player registration of the provinces, which means that if Ontario and Quebec collaborate, the rest of the country doesn't matter.

The priorities are so skewed, it's laughable. When we didn't qualify for the last World Cup, there was a CSA board meeting at which coach Steven Hart opened by saying that he was there to discuss the problems and to answer questions, and he would be there for as long as it took.

The answer? Dead silence, followed by one question, more silence, another question and "Thank you, coach. Now, moving on . . ." Then they moved on to the next item on the agenda: the sanctioning of an under-16 girls' team in the Maritimes. We've just been eliminated from the World Cup, and no one wants to debate or discuss what went on. Instead, on with the trivia!

In any other country there'd be discussion, a lot of long and heated discussion. Not in Canada. They just don't seem to *care*. Fire the coach, plug in another one and let's get on with things that matter. Maybe what's needed is a national World Cup committee. Get the amateurs out. The CSA should be governing, not picking national coaches. It should be concentrating on running rec soccer, where it excels.

Now let's look at the national team in the short term. When people ask me when the Canadian men should qualify for the World

Cup, my answer is always "The next one." The unspoken part is "*If
the players we have available decide it's all for one and one for all, as
we did in '84–'86.*"

We had one or two prima donnas and it was easy to tell who
they were—they weren't playing. Waiters' approach was simple:
cause trouble, show a me-first attitude and you'll sit or you'll be
gone. When I look at the present team and hear them slagging a
coach, I'm thinking, "That's where the problem is: you just don't *get
it*. You want to blame the coach when you should be looking in a
mirror. Do you think we qualified for the Olympics in '84 and the
World Cup in '86 on *ability*? No way. We were a bunch of lunch-
bucket guys who knew exactly what we had to do and played the
percentages. Wise up!" That has to change or we *won't* qualify next
time around.

So how do we qualify by design and not by accident? We need to
come up with a plan to get the best kids at an early age and do what
hockey does in this country. Hockey-playing kids know at any given
time exactly where they have to be to get the best chance to play at
their maximum level and get the coaching they need for a chance to
move higher. Their parents know, too, because they're hauling them
wherever they have to go.

In our game you can't do that yet. Everyone is claiming that
their way is the only way. There are private soccer academies making
buckets of money, but are they developing players? The kids probably are getting better coaching than they get with their club teams,
but it's a business, not a player development program.

The CSA approach to Major League Soccer is enough to make
me pound my head against the wall. There's a Canadian content
rule stipulating that two Canadians must be on each Canadian
MLS roster. The CSA wanted it increased. After much debate
MLS got it increased to three, and there's now a committee with
CSA and pro team representation that will determine when and if
the national talent level is such that the number can be increased
further. Otherwise, we could be adding Canadian players who actually could make our team weaker, which is ridiculous, especially

when you remember that it's the CSA that created the mess the game is in right now.

What the Whitecaps are saying is that we will invest money in player development and chart out a plan that will, after four or eight or twelve years (if you think in terms of World Cup four-year cycles), produce more Canadian players capable of playing at a high level, because up to now it's been hit-and-miss.

Is the rest of the world wrong? If young players are competing with and against players at their own or higher levels, they have to get better. What the Whitecaps believe is that the pro clubs have a responsibility to come up with a better way to produce better players, and once we start reaping the benefits of that program there won't need to be a mandatory Canadian quota. The number of Canadians playing on MLS clubs will rise on merit.

There are a lot of questions and no pat solutions. Is there an opportunity for a semi-pro second-level circuit across the country? Maybe not. Once you start laying out money for players, you have to think in terms of sponsors. I'm not sure that's doable right now. Maybe we have to restructure the senior amateur leagues to make them more viable.

Of one thing I am certain. Player development should have nothing to do with recreational soccer. They are two different animals with two different objectives. Think of it as a pyramid. The rec players, who make up the vast majority of minor soccer registration, are the base; the players with enough promise to think in terms of one day representing their country and/or playing professionally are the peak.

Where the rec soccer program goes wrong is that sometimes it starts thinking first of building club champions when it should be concentrating on making sure every kid who wants to play gets an equal opportunity, not just to stand on the sidelines but to *play*. That is where the CSA's responsibilities and effort should focus, not on picking national coaches and making national impact decisions.

I've been in the system forever, through minor soccer with

Grandview on up to Reading and the Whitecaps and the World Cup, so it's fair to ask: Why didn't *I* make changes? The answer is that when you coach, you coach. Your existence is based on results. If you don't get them, you don't coach.

The CSA has never understood that. When they hired Holger Osieck as national men's coach in 1999, I thought it was great—an experienced guy who was on Franz Beckenbauer's staff when Germany won the World Cup in 1990. Good move. Then they made him technical director as well as head coach, and I realized that was a *bad* idea, because one job is results-based and the other is about building a long-term program.

Look what happened. When Holger arrived he was hailed as a brilliant guy who won the Gold Cup in 2002. Then the team lost a couple and it was "Who *is* this guy? He doesn't know what the hell he's doing, and he's coming in and telling us how to develop players in this country?" Combining the two jobs doesn't work and never will.

As for Canada getting to the World Cup, let's not give up on 2014. Let's *try* to do it by accident, because we could get there, but doing it by design, and there has to be a design, it's never going to happen that quickly because player development won't be there in sufficient numbers. By 2018 we might be reaping some of the benefits, but by 2022, if we've done it right, we should be at the point where we're not complaining about the quality of the team we send. The trick will be to stick and stay and not make decisions that are reactive. Decisions made on emotion are always likely to be wrong.

Look at El Salvador, where they fire national coaches after two or three games. Even Mexico, for all its success, gets its result because it has good players, not because of its decision making. Lose a couple: bang, you're gone.

I love this country and this game. I want both to succeed. When Canada can be said to be one of the soccer powers, should that day arrive, I want it to be a two-fold tribute to our success on the world stage and our success at home, where the best players can reach their potential and the kids who just love to kick a ball around can do so on teams with their friends, learning sportsmanship, having fun and heading out for burgers, win or lose.

Let's make it happen. And while we're waiting, let's give a consoling hug and a supportive cheer to the national team that has built itself into a side to be reckoned with on the world stage, re-shaped and re-vitalized by a coach who, in a regrettably short stay, used fire and commitment to make it happen—Italy's Carolina Morace . . .

16

EQUALITY
AND OTHER MYTHS

"All animals are equal, but some animals are more equal than others."
—George Orwell, *Animal Farm*, 1945

When it came to women's soccer, I guess I was your average male chauvinist pig. Enjoy yourselves, ladies. If you want me, I'll be somewhere watching guys play the *real* game.

I have no excuses. My ancestral Italian chauvinism creeping in, maybe, an attitude where the women were supposed to cook and keep the house clean. Not unlike the male curlers' attitude when women took up the sport and some cantankerous old Scotsman snarled that when God gave woman a broom, He meant her to stay in the kitchen.

Then came the 1999 women's World Cup tournament.

When Sportsnet asked me to do colour commentary on its TV coverage, I went in with my biases hopefully buried but they were there nonetheless. It would be, I thought, like watching paint dry, a yawn-athon slower than continental drift. Sure, it was nice that the Americans got to host it, because they'd done such a great job with the men's World Cup five years earlier and they'd put on another great show . . . but, women's soccer? Come *on*!

More fool me. The more I watched, the more I enjoyed and came to appreciate it. As the tournament progressed and an amazing athlete named Mia Hamm led Team USA into the final against China, I came to realize that, power aside, the only difference between the men's and women's game was gender. In terms of desire, commitment, dedication, will to win and the ability of the great players to reach down for something extra when it counted, the women could stand with any team, any sport, anywhere. Listen to Mia Hamm explaining her game preparation: "I am building a fire, and every day I train, I add more fuel. At just the right moment, I light the match." Could Alan Ball have said it any better?

The USA-China final was played in the Rose Bowl and drew the largest crowd (90,185 screaming fans) of any women's sports event in history. They battled scoreless through regulation and overtime and were tied 4–4 in the penalty shootout with one shot left for each club. Briana Scurry blocked the last China shot, which left everything up to midfielder/defender Brandi Chastain, who coolly put the ball into the back of the net, raced up the field, threw herself to her knees, peeled off her jersey and clenched her fists as she flashed her sports bra. The picture made the covers of *Time, Newsweek* and *Sports Illustrated*. Pure show biz, and a pity in that it tended to put the focus more on the photo op than on the accomplishment, but it put the women's game on the American sports map as never before, and the shock waves radiated over the 49th parallel.

It wasn't that Canada had done all that well, or even gotten out of its group, drawing 1–1 with Japan and losing 7–1 to Norway and 4–1 to Russia. But the success of the tournament and the crowds it generated made it seem that the women's game was an up-and-coming sport, which meant Canadian soccer had to make a choice: be on the bus or be under it. Perhaps swayed by the world media fuss over Team USA and the Brandibra cover shots, the CSA acted with uncharacteristic swiftness. In a matter of weeks, the Canadian women's national team had a new head coach who demanded that the program be run independent of the men's and be given the backing for more games, more training, and no more of the condescending oh-they're-just girls-in-a-man's-game crap they'd lived with since the first national team was created in 1986.

A man by the name of Even Pellerud had the credentials to back it up. As coach of Norway's national women's team from 1989 through 1999, he led the club to a silver medal in the first women's World Cup in 1991, to gold in the second in 1995, and to a bronze medal in the 1996 Olympics. More importantly, he was a full-time coach with no responsibilities other than the nationals—a luxury the women's team had never experienced in previous seasons, being on or near the bottom of the CSA's priority list.

Some in the sport and the media who covered it were critical of Pellerud's approach, which was written off as "play physically, kick it deep and hope Christine (Sinclair) gets under it," but there was no disputing the initial progress. In 2003 Canada was playing for a World Cup bronze medal before losing 3–1 to Team USA. There was a hiccup in 2007 when Canada didn't get out of its group, but the following year brought a fifth-place Olympic Games finish.

In 2008, as Pellerud announced his retirement, someone at the CSA had a revolutionary thought: *It's a women's team. Why not find the best woman coach and turn the team over to her?* The choice, as every member of the women's team will tell you, was inspired.

Carolina Morace made the Italian national team in 1978—at age fourteen. Over her career she scored 105 goals in 153 games for the nationals and more than 550 in the national women's league; she played in six European championships and scored four goals, including a hat trick against Chinese Taipei in the first women's World Cup in 1991. In a five-year stint as Italy's national team coach, her record and motivational skills were so impressive that in June 1991 the Viterbese club of Italian Serie C1 was moved to do the unthinkable: it made her the world's first female head coach for a men's professional team. Media pressure quickly became intolerable and she resigned after two games—but think about it. A woman coach so highly *regarded* that she's wooed and hired by a Serie men's team? In *Italy*? How good would she have to be?

This good:

Christine Sinclair—"Carolina didn't just change our team. We joke that she changed *us* from athletes to soccer players. She demanded that we live a soccer life. She was *shocked* that some on our team didn't enjoy watching soccer. 'How can that *be?*' she'd ask. She's so passionate about improving and winning that she made it exciting to be a part of it."

Hall of Fame player Andrea Neil—"Here's the difference. She inherited almost the same group of players, but she came in with a methodology and a management style, which is easy to say, but it won't work unless the players buy into it, and they did, partially because they felt secure that no matter what her decisions, they'd always be treated fairly. She challenged them to change. They did it, and became an incredibly close-knit group with mutual respect. I played 18 years and it was never like this."

Kara Lang, in a statement she prepared for presentation to the CSA but was not given the opportunity to read—"Carolina Morace is the best thing that has ever happened to the women's program . . ."

Now, just like that, she's gone, resigning (did she jump, or was she pushed?) after the team's World Cup failure in Germany, where it looked totally competitive in a 2–1 loss to German's defending champions, utterly overmatched in a 4–0 drubbing by France that ended its hopes of advancement and disheartened in its final game 1–0 defeat by Nigeria. The showing dropped Canada's world ranking to eighth. But let's not throw the baby out with the bathwater.

Carolina's loss is a body blow to the program, but consider this. Heading into the competitition, Canada's FIFA world ranking had jumped to sixth. Its only losses in the previous two years were to the US, Germany and Sweden—first, second and fifth in the world, respectively. Dramatic progress has been made, and with the 2015 World Cup tournament to be played in Canada, the hope is that the women will keep their heads up, stay together and press on.

However, even before the World Cup in Germany there were signs that all was not totally well. In fact, things on the national front were so messy that the team logo should have been changed to crossed fingers rampant on Morace's face.

Last April the woman generally credited with revolutionizing the national program, citing differences with the CSA over the direction the program should be taking, announced that she'd be leaving after the World Cup. The players, weary of trying to live on the $1,500 per month they get from Sport Canada plus CSA appearance money for international games, were demanding bigger dollars. They were also lining up en masse behind Morace in the matter of who they want calling the shots on their national careers—Morace or the CSA's blazer brigade. It took a threatened team boycott to settle the coaching issue, Morace agreeing to stay through the 2012 Olympic Games in London. That raises another question. Her players went to the wall for her, and her answer is to walk out on them? Is it any wonder that they sometimes ask themselves if the end is worth the sacrifice?

You can see their point.

Members of the men's national team share their commitment and pride in carrying the flag and representing their country, but most of them are highly paid professionals. Do you think they'd do it for the Sport Canada stipend if those salaries weren't coming in? Yes, there is a North American women's professional league now, but teams are born and die so quickly they make the NASL look stable. The last time I checked there were seven. How many possible jobs is that?

The harsh reality is that at the world level the promise of the '99 World Cup hasn't yet come to pass. The hope is that the first-class show in Germany will rekindle the fire, but there are no guarantees—which means that, unless things change, the women currently on Canada's national side may face some hard choices.

"In a perfect world, yes, I'd be there in 2015," says Sinclair. "I so love this game, especially seeing the progress the national team has made over the past two years with Carolina, but the CSA situation and its lack of support makes it difficult to play on the national team at times. I've been doing it for eleven years and there's been so little progress on the support side. It's really frustrating . . ."

This isn't a whine or a poor-me complaint. There is no quit in Christine. In 2015 she'll be thirty-one and, assuming no injuries, still at or near the peak of her game. I'd bet the farm she'll be there. Despite the disappointment in Germany, the team could ride a wave of national pride over all its problems. But what does it tell you when Canada's greatest player—arguably its greatest *ever*—sees possible roadblocks in her fervent desire to represent her country?

There is a lesson to be learned. The women who'll carry our hopes have come this far basically on their own initiative. To move forward, their needs are identical to those of the men: a better development program, more emphasis on a system that will accelerate the process. The tournament in Germany showed that the women's game is growing and improving the world over. If we stand still, we're doomed.

That stint with Sportsnet at the '99 World Cup did more than make me a fan of the women's game. It also made me curious.

I knew the history of the men's team and the men's game in our country. Heck, I'd been part of it. About the women's game, I knew squat, and that was fine. I mean, it wasn't like it *mattered*. Now I knew differently and my ignorance nagged at me. How had this game developed? In particular, how did it get established in *Canada*?

So I did some checking and found that, with one exception, the women's game grew the same way the men's game had: game by game, crowd by crowd, triumph by triumph, stumble by stumble. It had its pioneers, developed its stars, and worked its way toward acceptance. But that exception was gigantic and at times must have seemed insurmountable. Nobody was telling the *men* they belonged at home.

Nobody said they shouldn't be playing this rough, tough, exhausting game. They were men, or boys who took to the vacant lots and parks and playgrounds as soon as there was a ball to be kicked. Of *course* they should be playing. Of *course* people would pay to watch the best of them.

A few weeks after our men's team competed in the '86 World Cup in Mexico City, a group of Canadian women made a twenty-hour bus trip to suburban Minneapolis to play an international game against the Americans. They'd had three whole days' training to get ready, and they knew what was at stake. If there was going to be a national women's program, they were told, then they had to do well against the Yanks to prove that Canada had the talent to make it worthwhile. Surrey's Geri Donnelly launched what would be a thirteen-year career with the Nats by scoring twice in a match whose result has been lost with time.

You want dedication? The women trained on their own, bought their own equipment and their own airline tickets to tournaments when fundraising fell short. There was no World Cup to shoot for, only a determination to play at the highest level they could.

Some tales of the rise of world women's soccer are unbelievable. Take, for instance, the Dick, Kerr and Co. Ladies, formed in Lancashire, England, during World War I as a morale booster for workers helping to produce ammunition for the troops. In 1921, when the team began drawing sellout crowds for fundraising games on the home parks of Liverpool and Manchester United to aid wounded troops, FIFA banned the team from FIFA fields because "football is quite unsuitable for females and ought not to be encouraged."

The Ladies played on and even came to North America in 1922, where the Dominion Football Association went all FIFA on them and refused to allow any games against any of our domestic teams. In the US they had to play men's teams (three wins, three draws and two losses) because there were no women's teams available.

What saved the game, I suspect, was simplicity and economics. In the 1920s, small-town Canada was the scene for pick-up games, often married women vs. single, viewed by the locals as nothing more than novelties and certainly not something to be encouraged or played in schools. Nonetheless, the games went on through the years as more and more women found enjoyment in the fundamental rule: if it moves, kick it; if it ain't moving, kick it until it does. As hockey equipment and rink rental expenses soared, baby boomers in ever-increasing numbers found pocketbook relief in this sport that required only a pair of boots.

Mostly, girls had to win spots on boys' teams. That changed with the formation of girls' minor soccer clubs, but it didn't come easily. It took time for the girls' teams to establish and develop. Girls who'd developed their skills playing on boys teams found the male-female split frustrating, and in at least one court case in BC, parents sought the law's help to allow their daughter to play on a boys' team. Interestingly enough, the boys' perspective on the subject could have saved the courts a lot of time. In the mid-'70s, a minor soccer manager asked his team of eleven-year-olds what they'd think if he signed a girl for the team. The boys huddled briefly, then asked the key question:

"Is she any good?"

From the mouths of babes . . .

A look at the CSA's registration stats for 2010 shows how much things have changed.

In 1973 there were only three girls' teams in British Columbia. Seven years later there were 317 clubs registered with the BC Girls' Soccer Association. By 2002, 42,000 women and girls were registered in BC alone, among 307,000 across the country. The 2010 national figures show 302,000 in girls' youth soccer alone and another 60,000 nineteen years and older. It works out to 43 percent of this country's youth players and 40 percent of its seniors. The Dick, Kerr's Ladies would never believe it.

There are still hurdles to be leaped, probably always will be. For the women, the biggest remains the question of acceptance by the soccer public, already earned but not yet awarded.

You know how that comes? The same way it does in all the major sports: star power. Name players with whom the game's fan base can relate. A female Messi, Ronaldo or Rooney. Which brings us, inevitably, to the force known simply as Sinky . . .

17

HOME-GROWN HEROINES

*"I don't think Canadians appreciate how good
Christine Sinclair really is. At the world level,
she's ranked in the top two—and, if anything, she's
under-rated."*

　　　　　　　　—Kara Lang, women's national team (ret.)

You could almost feel the wince across the phone line when it
was suggested to Christine Sinclair that she's become the face
of women's soccer in Canada, and this was weeks before the nose
on that face was broken by an errant German elbow in the opening
game of the World Cup. But it's true, and the title couldn't be in
better hands. Her numbers with the national team are staggering.
Heading into this year's World Cup competition she led Canada in
games played (158), starts (154), minutes (14,030), and goals (116).
She has been the team trigger almost from the day she made the
club at sixteen, scoring her first goal two days later as Canada beat
Norway 2–1. Only Mia Hamm tops her on the world career scoring
list, and Mia's 151 goals came in 259 games

Add her collegiate honours at University of Portland from
2001 through 2005 and her all-too-brief stint with the Whitecaps

women's team when national and school commitments allowed and you have a record unmatched by any Canadian soccer player—and yes, I mean male or female. And she still has years in which to add to her team and personal marks, which is why, when knowledgeable people discuss the current state of the women's game, she and Brazil's Marta—her teammate on the now-defunct Santa Clara, CA, Gold Pride of the Women's Professional Soccer League—are ranked one-two on the planet, and you can get arguments about the order.

So how did she get there? Hard work is a given, because no one gets there without putting in the time and effort. In Christine's case, maybe some of it was in the genes. Her uncles, Brian and Bruce, came out of the Simon Fraser University program, where Bruce was first-team National Association of Intercollegiate Athletics (NAIA) all-American in 1979. Brian played for the first three seasons with the original Whitecaps and six more with Portland Timbers, where Bruce also played for two years, so perhaps heredity was a factor.

The best Canadian player in soccer? No question: It's Christine Sinclair (L), seen here with national team clubmates Karina LeBlanc and Emily Zurrer (R). Christine led our women's Whitecaps side for three seasons, as she now leads the nationals. CANADA SOCCER

However, Bruce was a defender with 4 goals in his career and Brian, a midfielder/defender, finished with 23. Christine is a scoring machine, and always has been—except in her first year, which is understandable when you consider that she was four years old.

Her parents, Sandra and Bill, noticed how much she seemed to enjoy watching brother Michael play on a team her dad coached, and they enrolled her on the youngest team available, the under-7s. The team managed one tie and one goal in the entire season. Mind you, playing against ten-year-olds, six-year-old Wayne Gretzky scored only one goal in his first season and the rest of his career worked out pretty well.

There was another early Sinclair/Gretzky parallel. Both played baseball—Gretzky as a pitcher deemed to have major league potential, Christine on a mixed team with a steadily shrinking number of girls playing a game she loved. No. 99 decided on hockey. Faced with what she calls "the toughest decision of my life," Christine opted to concentrate on soccer (a grateful nation says "Thank you!!!"), primarily because the coach on her first provincial team (she was eleven playing under-14) said, "I can see you on the national team in a few years."

"That's when it hit me," she recalls. "It was like 'Wow! I can do this.'"

Good call, coach. Christine led her youth soccer teams to six league titles and five provincial championships, plus three high school league titles with Burnaby South Secondary. In nineteen appearances with Canada's under-18 and under-19 clubs, she scored 27 goals. She then debuted with the senior nationals in 2000 at the Algarve Cup competition and added three more. By then, she had an inkling of what her future might hold.

The '99 World Cup had given her a glimpse of the game on the world stage. US universities were offering scholarships. At the very least, she could use the game to get her education. And, wonder of wonders, it seemed possible that with the emergence of women's professional leagues she might even be able to make a living!

She sorted through the scholarship offers, narrowing it to

Portland, Nebraska and North Carolina. Portland won for several reasons: In terms of sport, soccer there was No. 1; there was no football team; the basketball team was average; and the women's soccer team regularly led the nation in attendance. Uncle Brian lived close by, the school was within long driving distance of home, so her folks could come to see her play (which they did on a regular basis) and she loved the city and the campus at first sight.

And then there was coach Clive Charles, "the best coach I've ever had," she says fervently, and a man she knew through her parents, who had rented a house from him in Burnaby. There was a comfort level, and later, when tragedy struck and Charles was diagnosed with terminal cancer, a way to say thank you. U of Portland had been to eight national final fours but had never gone all the way. In 2002, they won the title for him, 2–1 in overtime over Santa Clara with Christine scoring both goals in the last game he ever coached.

Christine's collegiate stats are staggering: 23 goals to lead all National Collegiate Athletic Association (NCAA) freshmen; 26 more as a sophomore; 23 in 2004 after red-shirting in 2003 to play for Team Canada in the World Cup; all-time Division I goal-scoring record in 2005 plus 2 goals in a 4–0 rout of UCLA for a second national title, which gave her a career NCAA record of 25 in tournament play; collegiate women's athlete of the year as a senior; consensus all-American every season; selection to the NCAA women's 25th-anniversary team; too many other awards to mention and, in her senior year, academic all-American of the year from ESPN as she graduated with a 3.75 grade point average in life sciences.

There have been a lot of firsts and a lot of memories in Christine's career. When she was competing in the 2008 Olympic Games in Beijing and living in the Olympic Village, the closing ceremonies in the Bird's Nest, surrounded by the great athletes of the world, fulfilled a dream of a lifetime. But ask her to name the best and there is no hesitation: it is that day in 2002 when they won the collegiate title for the man they loved and respected so much. A few months later, Clive Charles died at age fifty-one.

Now, about the face-of-the-game thing.

The wince, I suspect, comes from the fact that she knows the work that went into getting the women's game to its now-established place on the world stage, and that none of it might have happened had it not been for the country's first women's soccer pioneers, who were there when just finding a pitch to play on could be a problem and the ridicule level made it easier for the less-determined simply to put the game aside.

The Canadian Soccer Hall of Fame has honoured nine women who played, coached or refereed at a high level and had large roles in the development of the women's game, but the names Angela Kelly, Michelle Ring-Passant, Sylvia Burtini, Joan McEachern, Connie Cant, Sonia Denoncourt or Carrie Serwetnyk probably wouldn't resonate with today's fans. Helen Stembous, former player and current TV broadcaster, and Traci David, now coaching the women's team at University of Victoria and one of the builders of the collegiate game in Alberta, would have a better shot. But with today's

What a great feeling, to visit the BC Sports Hall of Fame and find your picture among the honourees. The '79 Whitecaps men were inducted in 1988, the '89 Vancouver '86ers in 2004, the Whitecaps 2004 women's team in 2007, and I made it in '92. KENT KALLBERG

sports world centred on stars and instant replay, the roads that got them there aren't given much thought, and that's a shame. Go to the internet and look them up. It's worth it.

One who recognizes that is Andrea Neil, elected this year to the Canadian Sports Hall of Fame and an assistant coach to Carolina with the women's national side with which she played in four consecutive World Cups. Her fifteen seasons (1991–2008, with one year out in '92 recovering from a motorcycle accident) and 132 Canada caps covered what she calls "growing up with the game while it grew, too."

Today's national team program is a 365-day-a-year enterprise. When Andrea first came on board there were only a few games per year or the program was shut down entirely, depending on time of year and amount of sunshine. The gradual growth shows in her record: twenty-nine caps in her first seven years, sixty in her next four. In a sense she was born too early, into a generation where the alternatives on leaving high school were simple: make the national team or go to college and pretty much forget soccer. There were no Canadian athletic scholarships, and the NCAA, where the programs were far more structured, hadn't yet begun looking north of the border. Today's best players can use the game for education and, as Christine has proved, the very best can make a living in the professional ranks, providing the ever-struggling pro leagues can win acceptance from an ever-fickle soccer public and build on a foundation more solid than the current quicksand.

I just hope that the bright young talents now blossoming on the national program don't forget to honour the ones who made it all possible and recognize the love and effort they poured into the sport to nourish its roots and help it grow. I know that I will always hold good thoughts for this team that worked so hard to earn that World Cup berth in Germany, and for the young woman who should have been there with them.

In 2002, fifteen-year-old Kara Lang became the youngest player ever to make the national team. Two days after her first appearance she got her first goal in a 3–0 win over Wales in the Algarve

Cup competition in Portugal and went into the FIFA books as the youngest ever to score in full international competition. She went on to a great collegiate career at UCLA and over a nine-year stretch became one of the mainstays of the national program.

I first met her in 2003 when we convinced her parents to allow her to come to Vancouver to join the women's Whitecaps. A sixteen-year-old far from her Ontario home? Not something we'd normally have considered, but her poise was even more apparent than her talent—and talk about competitive! Over three seasons with us she scored 9 goals in nineteen games. Then it was on to UCLA for a fine collegiate career while maintaining a key role with the nationals.

In all, Kara made ninety-two appearances for Canada and potted 34 goals, played in two World Cups, one Olympics, one Pan-Am Games and four CONCACAF championships. It was another of those fairy-tale stories that was supposed to have been capped by playing in this year's World Cup—in which, under the new Morace approach, she would have dropped back and become an attacking left fullback.

But the career had played hob with her right knee, leading to four surgeries including two ACL reconstructions. Training with the nationals in Brazil last January, she got the word from doctors that she had dreaded: "You're twenty-four," they said. "Keep playing, and you'll need a new kneecap before you're thirty-five." The decision was agonizing but she met it head-on, as she has done throughout her career. She announced her retirement.

A sad ending to a great career, but if I know Kara it will not be a full stop. She'll be involved somewhere, whether coaching or mentoring or setting up programs so other kids get their chance to compete at the highest level they can attain. She's a fighter, is Kara, and that's the thing about the growth of the women's game: when push comes to shove, the fighters have always been there in spades.

And that's the thing about our game: fighting *is* a part of it. Not the physical NHL kind. Fight in a soccer match and you're gone, and that's as it should be. The fight in our game in North America is to build the talent base, to improve the product and earn a share of the media spotlight, to make that product so entertaining that the soccer pitch, like the hockey rink, becomes the place to be.

That's been the women's challenge, as it will be ours as the Whitecaps step up into Major League Soccer. It's not going to be easy. Somebody—a Chinese philosopher, I think—said that the longest journey begins with a single step. We've taken that first one and we're in the middle of the second. There's been a stumble or two but we'll make it and, as that philosopher *didn't* say, getting there is half the fun. *That*, we've proved already . . .

18

HYPE, HIGH HOPES AND THE PAINTED LADY

*"Publicity is a suggestion made to a journalist to get
you a big story you hope he thinks was his idea."*

—Anon.

I t was 10 a.m. on a Saturday morning—March 21, 2009, to be exact. I was sitting in my car in the Global TV parking lot, windows rolled up, clutching my cell phone and letting out a yell that should have cracked the windshield.

A half-hour earlier I'd been live on camera doing what I'd been doing for the previous three days—trumpeting over and over again in newspapers and on radio and TV that the new Vancouver Whitecaps had been awarded a Major League Soccer franchise starting in 2011 and had just made 5,000 season tickets available to reserve *now* for a $50 deposit. I'd bombarded the media to the point where some said it was impossible to pick up a paper or turn on a radio or TV without hearing or seeing me. It had even been suggested by one or two that I back off and give it a rest.

But I couldn't do that. Not with millions of dollars invested in the new franchise when we had no way of knowing for sure how many people gave a damn. I'd given out the ticket office phone

First rung on the ladder to the top of the North American soccer market, our announcement in March 2009 that the Whitecaps had a new Major League Soccer franchise. WHITECAPS FC

numbers, urging people to call now and warning them not to wait because, with the soccer seating configuration at the new Empire Field not yet certain, we'd had to limit the advance sale to 5,000, which was a bit of a fib, because we did have a pretty good idea.

The projected on-camera confidence was a front. I had no idea how the campaign would be accepted. What if there was no interest? What if we sold only a thousand or so? What if we didn't sell any?

When the interview ended I spent ten minutes fidgeting in the car, then got on the phone to our CEO, Rachel Lewis. "I know it's early," I said anxiously, "but is there *any* indication?"

"You'll never believe it," she said. "We've sold 2,000!"

Hence the banshee yell. Oh, there was a ton of work yet to be done, but by Sunday night, two years before the new team would kick a ball, all 5,000 deposit opportunities had been snapped up. To us, the lightning early response was solid evidence that we weren't spitting into the wind, that the jump in class from Division II soccer, where we'd just completed our final season, was not unrealistic,

211

that we had a real chance to make it work—which was all the owner-ship group gambling their millions had ever asked.

I sat back in the car seat and, for what seemed the first time in days, allowed myself to exhale.

Marketing a sports franchise can be a chancy thing. North America is littered with the bones of football, baseball, basketball, tennis and soccer leagues and teams that were considered sure things to suc-ceed. We'd known that going in, and tried to do our homework in what for us was a two-tiered venture: keeping the USSF team viable and competitive enough to go for a farewell championship while simultaneously scouting the world—and, for that matter, the team we had—for players of a quality that would make us contenders in the major league now just over the horizon. It was a season-long tap dance.

Heading into the USSF season we had decided that, if we had players who might not be good enough for the step up to MLS when the time came, we would make roster changes as the season opened and again at the halfway point, bringing in talent with MLS potential even if they never saw the pitch that year.

Seattle Sounders, who'd joined the MLS a year earlier, had faced the same problem and admitted it was the toughest thing they'd had to navigate. Roster players' expectations were such that once MLS contracts were offered to some and not to others, the reaction of those who weren't offered contracts—even the ones who clearly weren't good enough—was "Hey! Why not *me*?", followed in some cases by an attitude change: if they weren't good enough for next year, why bust their asses in this one?

We got it done, and with a minimum of hurt feelings, I hope, but I know there were some. It just couldn't be helped.

In terms of promotion, attendance and fan enthusiasm for a start-up franchise, we had a couple of tough acts to follow. From the moment it opened the gates of the soccer-specific $62.5-million BMO stadium to launch its first MLS season in 2007, Toronto

FC had packed the place on a regular basis. The Sounders were in the same boat from Day One, which totally confounded me when I went to see a game and pump them about how the phenomenon had been hatched. We'd go down to Seattle for games, there'd be 1,500 people in the park and no one gave a damn. So what happened?

It turns out that the team's supporters' group—not unlike our own support group at Division II games—had taken it upon themselves to grow, to bring in other fans en masse. Adrian Haneur of the ownership group showed up for the first game hoping that the soccer atmosphere would be different from that of the local NFL and major league baseball crowds. Halfway through the match he looked at the crowd behind one of the nets and there was this mob, jumping up and down, chanting and generally acting like they were backing a team in South America or Europe.

So, the gauntlets had been tossed. All we could do was work, dream up a marketing program to catch the eye of customers old and new, and pray it caught on.

Our problem going into our promotional campaign was that we had nothing to sell—no team, no TV footage of signees, no stadium. We had to get creative. What our marketing people came up with was a thirty-day countdown with a different video each day featuring some well-known athlete or celebrity—Trevor Linden, Steve Nash, Lui Passaglia, restaurateur Umberto Menghi, rocker Bryan Adams—getting excited and counting down to kickoff when they'd be able to watch BC's new team in the greatest soccer league in North America. But that was just for openers.

On the campaign's first day, Vancouverites noticed something different about the statues of sprinter Harry Jerome and Man in Motion hero Rick Hansen: they were wearing Whitecaps jerseys. So were the two lions marking the entrance to the Lions Gate Bridge. Any local landmark that could be reached without an extension ladder was draped with a Whitecaps scarf. At five locations around metro Vancouver there were walls covered with scarves—about 2,000 all told—that fans could remove and keep. As each scarf was pulled away it revealed a printed reminder: "30 DAYS 'TIL KICKOFF!"

People loved them so much that by 9 a.m. our office phones were swamped with calls from fans annoyed because they hadn't been able to get one, so on the final day of the campaign we crammed the rest of the scarves into cars provided by Kia, one of our major sponsors, let people know where we'd be handing them out and took off. It was a gong show! We even had pleas via Twitter to come to specific locations so that people could dash out of work and get one.

Enter the painted lady, a lovely model named Andrea Stefancikova whom we featured in a video in which, ever so tastefully, she was seen having the Whitecap jersey painted on her torso.

We'd fretted a bit over how the public might react, but we'd run it past the members of our women's team, and with Kim Jackman, the woman who heads our marketing department, and they'd found nothing wrong with it. In European football, body-painting is a part of fandom. We were confident we were doing nothing wrong—and the public obviously agreed. We released one video per day on YouTube during the campaign, and on average they drew about 3,000 hits. The last time I checked, Andrea's had received some 400,000!

Not everything went right, however. A key part of our season ticket campaign was to include a team scarf with every purchase, with the opening-game ticket stitched to the scarf, the plan being that all these fans would then wear the scarves, which would look great in the stadium and provide great photo ops.

Unfortunately, we may not have done the best job of informing the recipients about that part of the gimmick. Some saw the ticket, thought it was a product tag for the scarf-maker—and ripped it off. On game day we had calls from fans screaming, "I don't have a game ticket!" Some dug through their garbage to find the fragments and pinned the pieces to the scarves. The rest we had come to the Will Call booth for replacements.

An unfortunate hiccup, that, but the entire campaign was put up for a marketing award, so I guess you could say it worked. Question was, would it induce people to check out our on-field product?

Game day: March 19, 3:30 p.m., Whitecaps vs. Toronto FC, when we find out whether all the work has paid off. I wake up, look out the window and it's pouring with rain. Oh, perfect.

But the soccer gods are watching. As I drive to the game it is merely cloudy. I go into the changing room for a while, step out-side—and the sun is shining. Better yet, there's a buzz in the air. People are lined up outside. When the gates open they head for the makeshift souvenir booths and they're strung out in lines 20 to 30 yards long waiting to buy a scarf or some other piece of club merchandise.

From outside the gates comes the sound of chanting. Now, I'd honestly thought on my trip to Seattle that our Division II sup-porters would have to step up their game to match that kind of enthusiasm. They must have thought so, too. About sixty of them who'd gathered at a bar decided to walk to the park as a group. By the time they got to the gates, their numbers had swollen to about 500, which wasn't great for traffic given the time it took that many to cross each intersection. Some people got perturbed. Me, I loved it. By then the media covering the match had heard about the fuss, so now the TV cameras were out covering the walk to the stadium. Yesss!

Things aren't perfect. Seconds before kickoff I see big gaps of empty seats. The ticket guys explain that hundreds showed up late and it took time to get them all in, but five minutes into the match the place is packed, sold out—and a strange thing happens.

The Southsiders are doing their chanting thing in their section, which we expected, but then, in little pockets scattered around the park, it's like the fans have decided that they're part of a soccer crowd, so they'd better start acting like it. Just like that, they're join-ing the chant, and the longer it goes on the louder it gets. What we had, on this day when we'd had no idea what the response might be, was a love-in.

Oh, yeah, the game.

We're back on our heels for a bit until Eric Hassli, the big

If size matters—and even if it doesn't—we knew we had a good one when we signed French striker Eric Hassli as our first designated player direct from FC Zurich of the Swiss Super League. WHITECAPS FC

Frenchman we'd signed out of FC Zurich as our first designated player, hammers one in. The crowd goes crazy. Toronto gets one back, but five minutes later midfielder Terry Dunfield, a Vancouver product clearly elated to be playing at home, puts us ahead again, dashes full bore at the stands and leaps into the crowd, where he is mobbed. It earned him a yellow card, I was happy to see. So were the media, who splashed the shot across TV screens and front pages the next day.

In the second half, we get two, they get one late, and we win 4–2. Fifteen minutes later, the fans are still in their seats. Nobody wants to see the end of a day that's turned storybook.

I try to get to the dressing room. Can't be done. The halls are full of fans trying for autographs, pictures, *any* memento of an historic day. I had a lump in my throat. Thirty-seven years ago, as an original Whitecap, I'd seen it like this. To see it again was special beyond words.

We've had our struggles. Expansion teams always do. But our fans have remained loyal, and they've come to know and cheer on this collection of newcomers working to come together on the pitch and to carve their own place in a province where hockey rules.

There are questions, of course. When soccer fans gather, when *aren't* there? But there is also a feeling in the air, a sense that good times are coming for a team that is setting down roots and rekindling the fires that warmed the old Whitecaps, their fans, and the city.

Who knows? Some day there could be another parade.

EPILOGUE . . .

So many memories . . .

I think of my folks—my dad now passed, my mom still alive and cooking—and how difficult it must have been for them to let their son go off to England to launch a new life before he was old enough to shave. And I wonder whether, facing the same decision, delivered in such an obstinate manner, I'd have had the courage to let my own son, Ryan, take the same plunge.

I believe so. I believe that during those formative years in the East Vancouver home, surrounded by love and laughter and a way of life that put family above all, enough of the old values soaked in for the apple not to fall too far from the tree.

In the blink of an eye, my baby boy has turned twenty-seven and my daughter, Sunny—the spitting image of her mother—is twenty-three. And I am proud to say that they have followed their passions. After a year spent working in a bank and learning that it wasn't for him, Ryan is in event marketing at Capilano College, goes to work in a track suit—it's in the genes—and plays and coaches a lot of basketball. Sunny spent two years at BCIT, is more into the arts and acting and has an interest in broadcasting.

They tried soccer. When Ryan was barely old enough to kick a ball I remember coming in from a backyard boot-around and telling Deanne, "He's never gonna be a soccer player." She took off on me the way Mom used to go after Dad. "You can't tell," she said. But I could, and I never pushed it. He played on teams I coached and took flak for not being good at it when his dad had *played* and was a *coach*, for Pete's sake. He was tall for his age—6'4" now—and we were both happy when he found basketball.

Sunny went into minor soccer at age seven. At the end of the second year she had a question. "Dad," she asked, "would you mind if I didn't play soccer?" She wasn't enjoying herself. In fact, she'd only started because she thought I'd want her to.

"Of course you don't have to play," I assured her. She hugged me a thank you, and that was that.

Sport is wonderful, but it's not the be-all, end-all. For 99.9 percent of those in any sport it is healthy recreation and should be

Celebrating Mom and Dad's 50th wedding anniversary, we gathered for what turned out to be the last shot of the entire family before Dad's death: Vanni (L) and me, Mom and Dad, Danny and Sam.
LENARDUZZI COLLECTION

Not exactly soccer gear, but what a thrill it was to take part in the torch parade for the Vancouver-Whistler 2010 Winter Olympic Games. The Olympic athletes gave us a tough act to follow. GABRIELLE BEER/IMAGE MEDIA FARM INC. FOR VANOC

enjoyed as such. Lucky sod that I am, I just happen to be in the other 0.1 percent. For her part in making that happen and for enduring the pressures and annoyances that have come with it, Deanne deserves some kind of medal.

In the twenty-nine years of our marriage she has always been my biggest backer. When I lost playing or coaching jobs it was always a question of how could I get back into the game. Move to Tacoma and play indoor for two seasons? Okay. Join the '86ers when the season didn't start for six months and we had no money and she was pregnant with Sunny? She went back into real estate and I played house mom with Ryan, which, for me at least, was wonderful. Now she has her own career as regional sales manager for western Canada with Lancôme Canada, the cosmetics and skin care giant, and she spends more time on airplanes than I do.

She knows how ready I always am to talk soccer with anyone who stops me, no matter whether we're shopping or out on the town. Sometimes she just moves on, but she understands that it's part of the business and, okay, that I love doing it.

The game is not my life. My family is, and always will be. But I still get up in the morning with a glint in my eye, plans and challenges whirling in my head as the great soccer adventure continues.

I am being paid to pursue my second love, and one song is lodged forever atop my personal hit parade.

"White is the colour; soccer is the game . . ."

Jump on in. And don't forget your scarf.

"Turn around and they're tiny; turn around and they're grown." The song had it right. Where *did* the years go? Just like that, our little kids Sunny and Ryan are all growed up. LENARDUZZI COLLECTION

INDEX